T0129565

Confronting Discrimination, Inequality and Racism in Search of Social Justice

LIFE EXPERIENCES *of a* FIRST-GENERATION MESTIZO (Filipino – Caucasian) "American"

Challenges, Struggles and Successes of A White Man in Brown Skin

My Story of Coping with Life and Discrimination as a First-Generation Immigrant

ALFONSO K. FILLON MPA

authorHOUSE®

AuthorHouse™
1663 Liberty Drive
Bloomington, IN 47403
www.authorhouse.com
Phone: 833-262-8899

Published by AuthorHouse 08/18/2020

ISBN: 978-1-7283-6963-1 (sc)
ISBN: 978-1-7283-6961-7 (hc)
ISBN: 978-1-7283-6962-4 (e)

Library of Congress Control Number: 2020914624

Print information available on the last page.

This book is printed on acid-free paper.

This book is dedicated to the brief life and memory of my son
Nathaniel Belli Fillon
October 27, 1985 - July 2, 2020

Contents

Preface

This writing and the information contained herein are based on my life experiences and perceptions to best of my recollection. Many of the foundations for my experiences are the result of observations correlated with the passing of information to me by first generation immigrant Filipino relatives, family friends, and associates. These are the memories from childhood and throughout my life; a span of approximately 70 plus years of life plus fifty years of my father's life and memories as a Filipino – Caucasian American, with a mother of Northern European ancestry; an immigrant father of Filipino ancestry. In most situations the noun Mestizo would generally be sufficient to explain my racial composition. However, it is my feeling that in this writing, given historical perspectives and experiences, it is important to advise and remind the reader that have had personal insight of a Caucasian but that there is a part of me that negated the personal reality of being Caucasian in the eyes of Caucasian "Americans". That negating element and force, was the fact that I had darker, even brown skin, black hair, brown eyes. It is that part of me that condemned me to being regarded as being only a brown Filipino and negating any acknowledgement that my mother was a blue-eyed, blond, Caucasian of northern European ancestry and recognizing me as an equitable American by White Americans. Thus, being a Filipino-Caucasian American provided a backdrop of scorn, rejection, related challenges and successes; experiences and feelings, that I desire to share with the reader. The life of being a "real" American was stolen from me by any and all with a different point of view; those who would put qualifiers on what being an American really was, and use those qualifiers to constantly remind me directly or subliminally, that I could never be, a "real American".

Some excerpts relative to treatment of me and my family by American Caucasians which I share through the book may seem harsh and make the reader feel uncomfortable. However, the experiences shared are simply truths and experienced situations; even opinions on experiences I was exposed to are shared only to enlighten the reader of the difficulties Filipino immigrants and their children, Filipino-Caucasian mestizo Americans, faced in the context of the wave of Filipino migration beginning mainly in the 1920's. I foster no blame, and no baggage, regarding adamant displeasure with attitudes of discrimination experienced by me and my family, or, my off-spring, pictures of which may appear in the appendix. Many Caucasian friends who have taken time to listen to my experiences at first, desire to feel bad for me or even express an apology. I share with you, the reader, that no apology is necessary, though of course, the empathy is appreciated for in the effort and feeling, empathy and feelings of acceptance is both conveyed and received. In my view, the expressions of hostile feelings and bigotry was endemic of a different - but poignant time in earlier American history. As this book goes to press in 2020, there is once again, dramatic social unrest throughout the United States engendered by incident of clear, visually recorded, instances of discrimination in community "Policing" throughout the United States. There have been race riots dating back at least 100 years. There is a bit of a difference this time compared to the early 1900's however. In the early 1900's and even to this date, there have been blatant efforts to hunt and "beat down" blacks and people of color (Reference hostilities toward Filipinos in Watsonville Calif. Jan. 19-23, 1930, https//en.wikipedia.org). The current social unrest and related demonstrations this time however, are by people of seemingly all races and ethnic colors seemingly focused on attempted assurance of equality in the application, if not the administration of criminal justice nation-wide. In other words, it could be said that this time, the heretofore discriminatory police "baton" reserved for people of color, may be getting too close to main street "real" Americans for comfort.

There is an irony in the dynamics of the current tone of rioting in the United States versus the rioting of the 1930's in Watsonville. California. Currently, there are many discussions and disagreements by much of the white population and other ethnicities as to the methods, motives and damage due to the rioting; the smashing of store windows, looting and the burning of businesses, police stations and police cars, etc. In the 1930's, (per records) a sign was posted by Whites in Watsonville, California riots to the effect: "GET RID OF ALL FILIPINOS OR WE'LL BURN THIS TOWN DOWN" (Courtesy bing.com/images).

I hope to see real improvement in the attitudes of fairness toward all people but in particular, Filipino-Caucasian American mestizos in "brown skin" who are seemingly underrepresented due to being viewed by one side of the Brown/White ethnic coin as "Not Brown enough to deserve a voice, recognition and inclusion as "real Filipinos" or noteworthy minority, and by the other side of the coin, "Not White enough" to be a "real American" and thus worthy of equality in social and business considerations.

I am proud to be an American and U. S. Military Veteran and tears up when hearing "America the Beautiful" being played and sang, for that is the America my father braved the trip across the sea to live in, become a citizen of, and give promise to the family he would foster.

I would like to thank the many friends, both Filipino and Caucasian, who encouraged me to go forward with my story of the challenges of growing up in the United States, being part Filipino and part Caucasian at a time when anti-Filipino racism was overt and in your face hostile; at a time when Americans were, more often than not, considered Americans only if they were of the White race.

I have been blessed by the friendship and mentoring of so many Caucasians over the years. Those friendships have helped to facilitate a more timely and meaningful assimilation into America for me, a bridge-generation mestizo. I would also like to take this opportunity to thank Ben Perlado, a first generation Filipino-American, for being a great friend and secondly for lending his valuable computer technical skills and assistance.

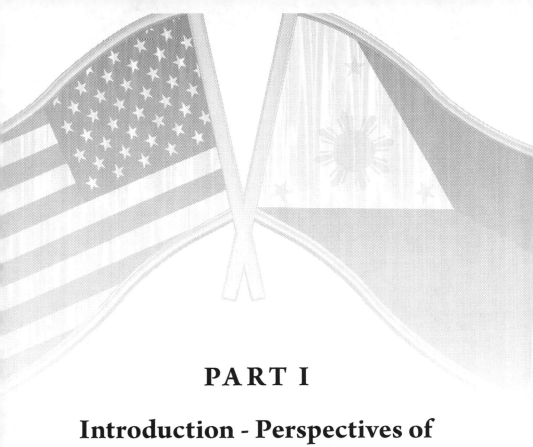

PART I

Introduction - Perspectives of Filipino-Caucasian American

Motivation for Documenting First Generation Perspectives of Filipino-Caucasian American

I began this journey by stating that I want the reader to understand that this is not an anti-white or "bad American book. It is not intended to be a "bad anybody" book. It is about occurrences and instances I perceived or experienced. At this point in my life I look at myself in the context of what I have become or not become having grown up in a great nation with so many opportunities for personal achievement. In doing so, I see that so many who were born of the American social classes at all levels and the many who were not American, have achieved and exceeded the basic standards of economic wealth, political achievement, exceptional social standing and super-personal and professional attainments. As I look back it causes me to reflect on my very humble upbringing and to critically look at, and assess, the reality of my struggle dating back over almost 70 years into a repressive society of that time compared to those seeming unlimited opportunities and support for those growing up in today's society. In the process of making comparisons I have to look with disdain on the inequities in American society at the period of time I grew up. Inequities which affected me and so many others like me, labeled "mestizos", (those of mixed race), and in particular, those of the "Filipino/Caucasian" racial mixture. Perspectives herein are mine based on my racial composition. I do not expect unanimous agreement from the reader with my perspectives, conclusions or opinions. These views, opinions and conclusions are accurate in my personal universe of experiences, perceptions, perspective, or thinking process. If anything, this could be considered a pro-Filipino book.

As I look about me today, returning to the geographic community in which I grew up, the Asian immigrant seems not so isolated. In businesses, schools, restaurants and shopping malls, it can even appear that the Caucasian, per "visual capita" could almost situationally be viewed as the minority in this and other communities. Times have changed but so has the environment, current laws and social experiences. Public non-acceptance of the Filipino or Filipino-Caucasian mestizo, public or even personal rejections or ridicule now carry penalties and even socio-political humiliation for the projector of most public forms and utterances of discrimination. Thus, our historical first-generation socio-economic hardship experiences and those of our predecessors may soon be lost forever if not candidly documented for historical reference and comparison.

It therefore dawns on me, as I watch my peers and others close to my age pass away, it is critically important that I put pen to paper lest the plight, struggles and experiences of the first or "bridge" generation Filipino-American mestizo be lost forever. Particularly because as I lecture and share the information and experiences with current or second or third or successive generation Filipino immigrants, they are skeptical that such overt discriminatory practices ever occurred or that such experiences ever existed in my community, maybe even in America; that the posting of signs such as "Positively No Dogs or Filipinos Allowed" was "uncommon. For those Filipinos still alive that witnessed these kinds of tangible discriminatory acts against themselves or other Filipino migrants, I ask that you document your remembrances and specific occurrences of them and share them with members of your families. I believe that sharing these experiences will lend to a greater appreciation of the immigration struggles of our forefathers and lead to a greater motivation to excel personally, socially and professionally. I hope that in documenting these experiences the newborn and current generation mestizos and others who might seem to take their social and political freedoms for granted may do so with the understanding that a price was paid by our ancestors. The reader who desires to get a deeper understanding of the price paid, will have a place to start with and understand that there was a time as relayed to be by my father, uncle, and others, when car loads "Americans" would conduct night raids of the camps where Filipino workers slept hoping to catch them off-guard and beat them up – even to hang them.

In view of the many nuances we are seeing in today's news periodicals, on audio and television, social and other multi-media avenues about hate crimes against minorities and particularly America's black population, racism appears still alive and well. I stop short of a judgement that it exists to the extent of "pervasive". In many cases, the "white American" of the early 1900's in America who viewed Filipinos in the United States as less than human, have transformed; transformed into Americans with different points of view or just bent on survival, or just protection of their own kind against other evils, real or imagined. Luckily for me, and many of us of brown skin, there are a good many who are genuinely supportive or just wish to stay out of the "fray". Many I know of brown skin just wish to travel under the radar and hope not to draw the ire of Caucasian down upon them. I know that story all too well.

I realize, accept, and believe, that we all have our own biases and prejudices. That to me is a God given gift necessary in the discernment of right from wrong. I believe it is how one applies those biases and the severity of hate, malice and infliction of pain that makes the difference of crossing the line. Unfortunately, being raised as a Christian, the element of social hypocrisy comes into play. In this context, one need only access "Filipinos unfavorably depicted in (American) media" on your respective electronic search engine to view the various negative portrayals of Filipinos as inherently bad, savage, and an out of control burden to the American political psyche upon purchase of the Philippine Islands from the Spanish for $20 million dollars circa 1898.

The writing that follows is a macroscopic narrative in the life of one Filipino-Caucasian "American" mestizo within the context of his (my) birth and my assimilation into the American community. The American community which is the basis of many of the experiences I make reference to is Stockton California. Stockton, was and still is, a small town in the central delta region of California with a thousand miles of waterways in the region of the state's central San Joaquin valley approximately 50 miles east of San Francisco. In the 1930's, 40's and 50's this fertile area was inundated with agriculture. Arriving in San Francisco off the boat, a good number of Filipinos found their way to the central California valley relying on agriculture for their daily livelihood and as an economic bridge to support their transition into America; my father was one of these. In a socio-psychological context, there is a lot to examine, and a lot to deduce from the information I share for anyone who may want to study the evolution of the Filipino and the origin of the Filipino - Caucasian Mestizo.

As I put pen to paper to first record events of the past and secondly to pass personal experiences of the past as well as those from personal recollections. I cannot help but be saddened; saddened that I did not take advantage of the many opportunities I had to delve into the experiences my father and other Filipino immigrants had as a part of coming to America. I would have liked to discuss the dynamics of how they made the decision to come to America. I would have liked to ask the question of just what motivated them to come to America; just what exactly caused them to make the decision to come to this foreign land in the first place? Further, once the decision was made, what was the process each Filipino put into operation to facilitate their personal voyage to America. I know that my father's family put money together to pay for the trip, but how did Filipinos go about making the arrangements. In my father's family, three brothers personally and separately made the trip with one arriving on the east coast.

For that one brother, that ended up on the east coast, life in New York city turned out to be too much of a challenge for him. He was not easily bullied by Americans without a willingness to take matters into his own hands; I have been told by family that a "bolo" or "itak" in Tagalog (Philippine type cousin to the "Bowie" knife but shaped and weighted for chopping, personal defense and offense) was always close by in his cab. Seemingly, this "monkey" was not one without fangs. I was also told and the story verified, that my grandmother sent emissaries to New York with instructions to return him to the Philippine Islands "post haste"; that the American dream would not be in the cards for him. "And so, it was"; my uncle returned home to the Philippines. In other words, it was said that my uncle was quick to unsheathe his bolo. Ironically, the "bolo" was one item I purchased in Subic Bay from curio vendors who had native products for sale when I was in the Philippines in route to Viet Nam. Upon return to the United States, I presented the bolo I purchased in the Philippines for personal use to my father who cherished it to his dying day.

As a Filipino-Caucasian Mestizo youth, I was one of those students that teachers would say of to my parents, "he is very bright", "he should be a doctor or lawyer". When students are identified as such in terms currently, scholastic support and financial grants, scholarships and related resources seem inevitable today's scholastic world. In contrast however, next to no financial resources were available to the minimum wage mestizo children in the earlier school systems in which I grew up. As I look back, I am aware of numerous other mestizos who were as sharp or sharper than I, yet had to settle for convenient localized professional attainment as in education, law-enforcement specialties, and generally, low to mid-level civil servants, etc. I am not aware of any as of yet who were supported by the "system" to become Ivy League University Presidents but I have hope that the Filipino and the Filipino-Mestizo American will soon break out of the box. I feel that many had the ability, but the system at the time did not support "breaking out of the box". If such was a matter of personal choice, such professional attainment is certainly honorable and commended. Perceived security of a civil service job is what my father was willing to accept for me as a first- generation American son of an immigrant. It is why my father tried so hard to keep me from getting into trouble in school or elsewhere. However, "my bone to pick" with this acceptance is that it is my personal opinion that much of this during my youth was a matter of outright imposed mental or subliminal conditioning of brown skinned people by "Americans" and the American stereotype of Filipino-American Mestizos and other children of color. As I share again later, becoming a police department commander, fire department chief, university president, governor in America was not encouraged for Filipino-Caucasians by Americans, but in fact, was discouraged. There were those of the Filipino bridge generation, of financial means or not – who were able to break the bonds for one reason or another and succeed. For my peers who likely endured many prejudicial hardships to attain higher positions, I commend them; their stories deserve to be told; I encourage them to tell their story; mine is only one. Even in America today, however routine attainment in corporate America by those of Filipino descent (mestizos) is not the norm.

I provide the following example in hopes that it will clarify the essence of my feeling on this matter of social difficulty for many, if not most, minorities and specifically, the Filipino American or Filipino-Caucasian mestizo. During a recent televised national pandemic briefing from the "White House" to the American public regarding manufacturing company production of products with which to fight the Corona Virus 19 pandemic, approximately eight manufacturing company Presidents/Chief Executive Officers (CEO) were called to the podium by the President of the United States to announce to the American Public what their company performance was and how many hundred thousand "widgets" their respective company(s) were producing to aid in the fight against the pandemic. One by one, each CEO went to the podium to make their presentation. I noted that the first seven CEO's were male whites. The eighth CEO was a female - white! It struck me that out of eight executives running major manufacturing or production companies none were minority and of course, not a one was of Filipino heritage. It is in this context that a haunting reality from the past causes me to feel that little has changed over the seventy-six years of my father's life in the United States or the seventy plus years of my life in terms of those of Filipino heritage assimilating into the American mainstream and becoming corporate leaders! We still have a long-ways to go! If anything, this is an encouragement to "breakout" of the mold from main street to "power broker" or from Main Street to Wall Street". I share later, however, that breaking out of the mold in bureaucracies is not an easy process. First, it takes a special person to make the attempt to break traditions, break out of the mold, manage subtle to fierce racist recrimination and then to put themselves, and their loved ones in jeopardy in the process. Secondly, there has to be a tangible opportunity, either in fact or through manipulation of the system, for the Filipino-American to aspire to. Simply put, there are not usual opportunities for "such people" in the eyes of type A American personalities such as is prevalent presently in American Government. As a matter of fact, none have appeared up for cabinet level posts nomination or confirmation, or even considered for nomination to the United States Supreme Court to date. At the rate of assimilation into power positions in the bureaucracy we are going, I unfortunately, rather doubt any will be in my life-time, regardless of reason or anyone's rationalization as to why not.

It is my hope that this written work will offer a foundation for personal introspections and be warmly embraced by the members of Filipino communities, organizations, American educational institutions including ethnic studies classes, sociological and psychological disciplines, law enforcement and court systems as a bridge for understanding a unique faction of society and the candid perspective it offers. I hope that the experiences shared here of a Mestizo's life and struggles can demonstrate the hidden complexities he or she has evolving into being an American and the unique struggles of most of us in trying to do so. I believe and have been told by others, knowledgeable of this work, that in year 2020 America, there is still a lack of clarity and understanding by many Americans, politicians, bureaucracies, business organizations and educational institutions and the like as to bases of unrest and frustration as to the status quo of racism in practice that permeates the air and the minds, even of authoritarian service providers; service providers with the mentality that, even if the public is watching, keeping your knee on the neck of people of color for a second longer is okay, even necessary because in their minds; especially since people of color are not Americans anyway and thus, "they got no justice coming". As I write this book, a thought has awakened within me. I am still empathic and fearful that Filipinos still seem to be lacking in massive voice representation and ability to powerfully organize, protest and create the fear in perpetrators of injustices to Filipinos such as the black population has embodied when injustices are perceived or perpetrated. I just know, that as a youth I felt helpless where overt, aggressive, discrimination was concerned relative to me, members of my family (white and brown) or my associates of color. I never liked the idea of flying under the radar to avoid making waves.

I still have vivid memories of a Caucasian girlfriend who after several years of a close relationship berated me because of my relationship with, and affinity for, my "minority friends". This revelation occurred and was dropped on me like a "bombshell" one night after a company party and her consuming perhaps one too many glasses of wine. My point here, and I repeat throughout this book, is that racism is pervasive, whether in personal relationships, in organizations, or at the local restaurant; if you are of color or, have made a choice to be with a person of color, be "On Guard".

Foot Note:

As this book goes to press, once again, thousands of buildings and business are burning uncontrollably throughout the nation, not just at the hands of black population's backlash against alleged white oppression and murder but this time, seemingly by other minorities; the poor, the disadvantaged or anti-bureaucratic movements. The jury is still out, figuratively and literally, on validity of motive and cause and effect. It is a given that to me, that some destruction is rage and, some subliminal to conscious retaliation related; other acts are associated vandalism, provocation or disregard for others.

PART II

Summary of Life and Views of a Filipino/Caucasian American
(Overcoming Immigration and Racism Bias in America)
"Another Monkey"

Growing up as I did, a first or "bridge" generation brown-skinned person in a predominantly non-multicultural tolerant community in white America, presented many assimilation challenges. Growing up in such a community, Stockton, California, a mid-size city in the central valley of California as a person of mixed Caucasian and Filipino heritage known as a Mestizo had discriminatory interactive and communal acceptance challenges all its own. Living each day of my childhood, growing up and attempting to assimilate into such a society presented many additional socio-psychological challenges separate and unique for an individual referred to as a "mestizo!"; a person of mixed race. It was not unusual to experience a day where I would hear myself referred to as "another monkey or "damn brown bastard" in my community or even when passing through a white neighborhood on the way to school or have a white person "flip me the bird or middle finger" for no apparent reason. It was not uncommon in school or in public, to be referred to by physical characteristics such as "slant eyes' versus my given name. In retrospect, I now realize that I heard, and was the recipient of, racial slurs associated with numerous non-white races and mixtures given that White Americans of that era, had limited association and learning about other races. They generally did not know the difference between a Filipino and a Mexican, Indian, Arab, Eskimo, etc.

The personal story and perspectives I share here are from my own particular viewpoint: the experiences, assertions, conclusions and pain as well as a whole host of descriptive adjectives are fundamentally mine and relate to my own feelings, perceptions and sentiment. This work also provides a perfect opportunity for understanding, mental remediation and/or behavioral adjustment techniques for the readers who may find themselves in similar immigrant conflict or difficulty. Again, for clarity, the following are my premises:

- This presentation is based on my personal experiences, opinions, conversations and conclusions.
- My thoughts, opinions and conclusions are not intended to exclude conclusions and experiences of others; each are expected to be independent and different

- I do not expect concurrence; there is ample room for theoretical and philosophical divergence or disagreement;
- Some of the divulgences may be ugly and make the reader uncomfortable. However, none are intended to focus on, accuse, demean or insinuate responsibility of the reader or the listener for those on audio. However, growing up in Stockton in the late 40's and 50's it was not uncommon to hear myself or other Filipino or Mestizo children, if not adults, referred to as "just another F------ monkey". I am however, astounded when I hear some Filipinos now who grew up in those days reluctant to acknowledge this ever occurred to themselves or others. However, in addition to my personal experiences, I myself, sorrowfully heard categorical referrals to anyone of "our kind" in such a manner and was also told of these occurrences by those "Manongs"*, relatives and associates who initially migrated here and have now passed on. Based on scuttlebutt (rumor) however, I am not sure how many offenders did or not fall victim to the butterfly knife, bolo, Saturday night special, etc. - or should have. Even for a Christian, of which most of my family is or was before passing, such indignities should not have had to be tolerated.
- Any ugliness, discomfort, psychological deviation from acceptance, is a result of my environmental exposures and personal memories and reality; there are no desires for any form of reparation or compensation or apologies to be received;
- There is also a silver lining and constructive enlightenment in having had to cope with racial discrimination and prejudice over a life time. In the military service, I was told that if a bad experience doesn't kill you, it will make you stronger. There were times however when my tears of disappointment, anger or disgust at the time, might as well have killed me.
  *A Filipino term of respect for the elderly or revered Filipino males
- I have chosen to write about my experience of exposure to prejudice and racial discrimination for several reason. First, it is first-hand experience generally suffered by many off-springs

of the Filipino migrant who had children of a mixed race in the United States. Secondly, after many years of personal feelings of contempt for the feelings of discrimination, bias and ridicule I am able to reflect and articulate the experience first-hand in an objective and intellectual manner - particularly, since as mentioned in the preface, few modern immigrants will be able to relate to this history. Time and laws have changed, even some attitudes though discriminatory racial inner thought and biases still exist! Finally, given the many changes since arrival of my father in the U. S., current immigration conflicts and civil unrest in our world at the present time, year 2020, perhaps this is the time to "pick the scab" one final time to ensure the past, present and future generations of Filipinos and Filipino-Caucasian mestizos are aware of their history, the plight and often graphic unpleasantries experienced by those who preceded them to, and in, America.

–   Finally, growing up at a time when racism was fresh and imminent greatly impacted how I viewed myself consciously, and subconsciously in that context, for the rest of my life; affecting most all decisions I made relative to pursuing life in that world and what ramifications might manifest themselves throughout my life because of it.

Some narratives in this book about growing up a Filipino-Caucasian mestizo I had the opportunity to share for discussion April 28, 2019 at the Filipino American National Historical Society Chapter in Stockton California. I am deeply appreciative of the Filipino American National Historical Society of Stockton for that opportunity to share this information at a recent consortium of community attendees. I also wish to express my gratitude to Lois Magaoay Sahyoun, herself not only a mestiza of Filipino/European descent, but also a migrant to the California Central Valley from Alaska, for inviting me to join her as a presenter on this subject. It was her interest and desire for public expression and insight into the need to express our point of view given the fact that the experience of mestizos of the Filipino/European mix might be overlooked though different than that of other mestizo mixtures and other ethnic combinations whom heretofore have been perhaps more visible and/or vocal.

The Filipino-Caucasian (mestizo) is seemingly an unknown entity in America's "American" society of forefathers. The Filipino-Caucasian was and still seems to be, a person without a defined identity; a face and group without recognition or even acceptance in American society. There is not even a classification on racial identification screening documents that provides an accurate classification. Most Filipino-Caucasians are left to select as the closest classification, "Pacific Islander". These Mestizos have, by all demographical elements, been a silent group of people who, by all appearances, seemingly have hoped that by following the American traditional dictates, or proverbs of "hard work pays off", experienced just the opposite in many cases. They were, and we are, still commonly viewed as a simple people with no assertive representation in federal law or local policy or even "benevolent organizations. In "Images from the Past, Stereotyping Filipinos, (Melissa Flores, Santa Clara Undergraduate Journal of History, Vol. 9 Article 8,) the author cites "Stupid", "Morally Inferior", "Savages", as words that Americans widely used to describe Filipino immigrants in the 1900's through the1940's and beyond. My experiences in the late 1940's and 1950's were a close reflection of the same referent adjectives. By most accounts, the Filipino-Caucasian has posed a physical threat to few if any. I have been told by Caucasians, male and female, that the mixture makes for a person with handsome or pretty features which incites jealousies for some. I have observed and concluded that our cultural orientation in America has been simply one of respect for persons, person's property and family, authority and government. It would appear that the Filipino immigrant was appreciated as a domestic or farm worker as long as they stayed "in their place" and were not a threat to the comfort level of the white population. Not being threatening however, seemingly equated to low pay, "little to no recognition or social progress" and an expectation of staying away from "our white women" as white Americans would phrase it.

As a matter of comparison however, I believe and have observed that the vociferous threats of the Black Power movement of the 60's, though reviled by white Americans and perhaps others, has gradually paid off to some degree for many of the Black-American culture. Contrary to the Asian cultures, who in my opinion have suffered second class citizenship in silence, there were frequent T. V. programs highlighting Black Power movement assassinations of police, anti-establishment movements, sit-ins, bombings and detective stories all focused on trying to capture the alleged anti-establishment culprits as highlighted in "Dirty Harry" and other movies. Black American advances did not come easy however. There was the price of public beatings, shootings, jail and prison sentences; even executions. It appeared that burning businesses, communities, assassinating community leadership and authorities was necessary to gain, if not extort, social advances and validity as worthwhile Americans worthy of being now highlighted in movies and finally now shown in almost all advertisements, T. V. commercials and social settings on the television screen. As I look back in Black history, I recognize the many gains made by the NAACP (National Association for the Advancement of Colored People) founded in 1909 by a coalition of Black and White activist to secure the political, social equality and essentially eliminate race-based discrimination. It seems that about every twenty years, our society is reminded of graphic indignities and atrocious behaviors that ignite the flames of racial bias and injustice. As this book goes to press, we are again reminded that all is not well in terms of American racial attitudes and behaviors. This time however, the reaction is more multicultural and multi-color. This time could be different but the jury of history is still out. Only time will tell.

Many readers may disagree with me when I share my wish that my father, I, and others, could have been the benefactor of such a group, a National Association for the Advancement of Filipino People able to martial thousands of protesters at the hint of injustice to Filipino people, of which there have been many such injustices (perhaps in time, we will become bolder, more dramatic, more dramatic, even more feared for political power and clout). I think Larry Itliong, labor organizer, came closest to achieving this power advocacy mission but I am, in retrospect, wondering why seemingly, he did not get overwhelming support from the brown community. I can only surmise that there was reluctance for a myriad of reasons, one being to avoid bringing attention to oneself and thus further inflaming the ire of the "white" man, good ole boy club or "establishment". In that regard I think of something my mother said to me as I was growing up and agitating, - "If you don't take a stick and stir it, it won't smell.".

The Filipino/Caucasian is however, not as conspicuous, assertive and demanding of rights as they could have been, in my opinion; I have no answer as to the reason for the passivity. There is seemingly little data driven research on this passivity. It is my experience, observation and perception and continued opinion that those of Filipino descent are not being recognized or sought after as existent or as a meaningful part and contributor to the American landscape, cinema and society as they should be. Growing up, I sometimes wondered if the seemingly too passive Filipino-Caucasian American was destined by culture to be too timid to pay the price for achieving blatant notoriety; Filipinos Americans demanding daily exhibition before the American public and in each American living room nightly on television as newscasters, show hosts, advertisers, actors and actresses, etcetera; During recent national unrest (May 2020 George Floyd death in police custody) I did observe one Filipina, identified as Elita Loresca, Journalist, Meteorologist, reporting related rioting news from ABC13 Houston, Texas. Originally from the Philippines, married and a mother she has moved extensively throughout the United States to further her career opportunities now with a net worth $5 Million. Ethnicity *"Asian"* (note the generic category of ethnicity as given - *"Asian"*). (Source: Celeb Body Stats, Nov 14, 2019) "Kudos" are in order.

Even now in America (year 2020), I notice that there are numerous commercials where there are black and white interracial couples and families used to advertise products. However, I have not seen advertisements where Asian-Caucasian couples are used in advertisements. I believe this observation to be pretty accurate where American companies and advertising agencies and mentalities are concerned. I ask myself, why are we missing from this scene? At the moment however, it seems we are missing that voice and muscle that demands recognition "or else". We are still seemingly content to "fly under the radar".

I periodically ponder the question and wonder, are we still stuck in the 1920, 30's, 40's and 50's by choice or by American attitudinal stereotyping and casting as a "simple" non-threatening people without worthwhile public recognition, interest and public appeal??? I see some of this performer showmanship and pride happening on a small scale in the arena of sports, thanks to boxer Manny Pacquiao of the Philippines. However, when he takes his fame, our sentimental association and recognition of the Filipino back across the "pond" with him, then - there is left a quiet void. We are left with memories of our boxing heroes of the 1930s, 40s and 50s, as touted by my father such as boxers, "Flash" Elorde and "Speedy" Dado, and Roman Gabriel, quarterback of California based national football team. I would have liked to grow up having more active Filipino idols and icons fighting discrimination prevalent around us at the time, versus idols passive in history books (no disrespect intended); life may have been easier from any number of viewpoints in the 30's, 40's and 50's, like me. Still, I have faith that, with the contributions of our people who have made it and actively campaign for Filipino equality, or are in the process of being successful, we will eventually get to our own "promised land".

Fast forward to the present 2020. I note an important comparative observation – there are now many advertisements on television that include Black members of society in them. I admire the progress made from obscurity to an imminent presence. Unfortunately, there are still very few advertisers that use Filipinos or Mestizo Filipino–Caucasians or even feature them independently in commercials as representative of American households or businesses. Persons appearing of Asian ethnic origin seem to have a "generic" cultural projection -if at all - representing all Asian ethnicities or are gladly viewed as exorbitant comedians. Such was my personal reaction to a relatively new theatre movie "Crazy Rich Asians"; my Caucasian neighbors however, found it hilarious and recommended I go to see it. I did go to see it and did not find it conventionally funny. I do not know how the ethnic group it represented felt about the culture being portrayed in such a manner. However, relative to the experience, I did not hear of protest or boycotts and the like from the Asian community demanding to be shed in a more rational light - so perhaps it was a rational and acceptable portrayal; I am not in a position to conclude anything beyond my personal conclusion and in that vein, I must admit that I am no recognized movie critic. I am aware that it did get billed and recognized as a movie of great acclaim. I guess that some acclaim is better than none; I did not go to see it a second time to validate or invalidate my opinion. I will bow to and commend the effort made and stick to detective movies. I will leave the hilarity of it all for my Caucasian friends to laugh at as quality entertainment.

Historical Brown Movement comes to Campus - circa 1968

The Brown Beret movement of the 60's on my college campus founded by Dr. David Sanchez in southern California to resist discrimination, harassment, inadequate schooling and improve healthcare. seemingly composed of mostly individuals of Mexican-American descent and other brown sympathizers. However, humble its beginnings, their assertiveness combined with the individual and collective aggressiveness by other association was the foundation and basis of greater visibility; more job opportunities in the mainstream workforce, movie and television parts and today representation in most every product advertisement on television as well as news anchors, weather reporters as well as other soap opera and television program castings. I remember my loosely affiliating with Mexican-American and other Filipino mestizo friends, and myself in junior college in Stockton in the late 1960s, as Brown Beret sympathizers and a time of social awakening, looking for causes to protest at the time – one of which was to protest the throwing of rice at weddings. I am not sure of the position in the organization of the leader at the time but the recognition of a Brown group rally in the Forum at the time was excitement enough.

I can speak only from my personal perception and opinion but from that perspective it appears to me that the American Filipino Mestizo and particularly the American Filipino Mestizo of European descent, still has a ways to go if we are to take our rightful places as viewed contributors to America, of being citizens of value and being sought out and recognized for our accomplishments and social potential or recognized and portrayed as members of existing households and families in America. I and other Filipino – Caucasians bridge generation Americans have a story to tell for our descendants. Again, this is only one among many others.

I would like to thank my parents for their personal devotion to bringing up a child (me) during the post "Depression" and providing a moral and spiritual foundation during some hard times. I would also like to thank my friends and mentors, Lois Magaoay Sahyoun herself a Mestiza and Dr. Richard Tenaza, PhD Professor Emeritus University of the Pacific, also a Filipino-Caucasian American, each, for their encouragement in awakening and evoking this personal life experience memory and recital in me. Due to the subject matter of this book, I want to acknowledge and appreciate my many white friends past, present and future who were open minded enough to accept me as I am and extend me their friendship and support in life's endeavors.

An Important Note to the Reader

As a matter of foundation in this material, I must provide the reader with the understanding that at the time of my father's migration to the United States and during the course of my childhood and preadolescence, people of brown skin were generally not regarded or referred to as Americans regardless of whether they were naturalized citizens or actually born on continental United States as I was. In that time, you were only regarded as an American if you were "white". It is in the context of that attitude and time period that I grew up and the basis from which I share these experiences and perspectives.*** Many Filipino youth of today are shocked and in disbelief to find out that there was a time in their American community, when they would almost surely be yelled at as "hey monkey" by passing motorists or other youth - in the streets, especially in north Stockton, California. I later refer to a time when Filipinos would not be shown residential property north of Harding Way.

What I share here are my experiences and my perceptions as I experienced them. It is not meant to invalidate in any way, differences of experiences, perceptions, conclusions or seeing this through "other eyes".

Again, something for all of us to think about and take to heart.

***As this book goes to press, the nation's people are protesting by the millions, relative to the death of a black man, George Floyd, who passed away during the process of being taken into police custody. Where were the protesters when Filipinos were being hunted down? The protesters of that time were not out to seek justice for the immigrant Filipino or the Filipino-Caucasian mestizo with brown skin. No, they were out to protest the existence of the Filipino in America. I now see many of the Black-American population demanding recognition, equality and equal opportunity, movie contracts etc. I am a little disappointed that I am not seeing similar demands and expectations from Filipino-Americans, or even more broadly, those Americans of all Asiatic ethic origins.

Poet Martin Niemoller is attributed the following quote:

> "First they came for the Jews, but I did nothing because I'm not a Jew. Then they came for the socialist, but I did nothing because I'm not a socialist. Then they came for the Catholics, but I did nothing because I'm not a Catholic. Finally, they came for me, but by then there was no one left to help me." I champion the cause of activism and proactivity for the Filipino-Caucasian mestizos and Filipinos in general.

Something for all of us to think about and take to heart.

Some Caucasian friends my age say they never saw or were aware of racism and prejudice against Filipinos when they were growing up. My response to that is that you had to be looking for it in order to see it; you didn't look for it if you didn't feel it. When you were the one being discriminated against, you generally knew it was there before you saw because if you were prone to be a victim of racism, you had a sixth sense that could sense it in the air, in how someone looked at you, in what someone said to you and in what they did not say.to you, you could grasp it in the choice of words, adjectives, verbs and pronouns used to communicate at or *to you*, not *with you.*

On numerous occasions I have encountered such communication from individuals I encounter where you know you have been communicated with in an off the wall way and know it is happening. At times, I have had mates or friends with me when it is occurring: those associates generally do not understand what is happening, but at times, such demeaning situations are so smoothly communicated that your friend or partner just don't get it. It is as though they are conveying to me, I have chosen to teach you "American" speak today, dummy (not English).

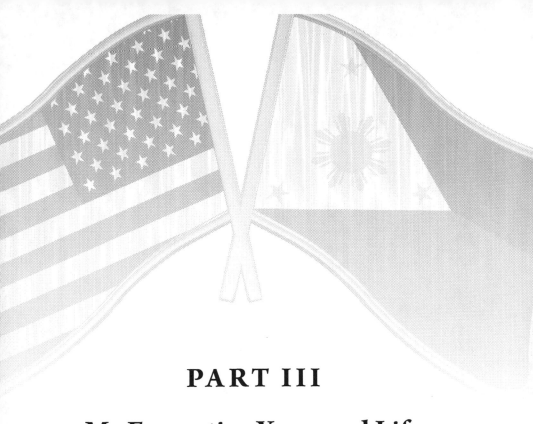

PART III

My Formative Years and Life as a Filipino-Caucasian in Small- Town America

I was born in the year 1946 in Stockton, California at St Joseph's Hospital and raised in Stockton, California. My parents, father of Filipino heritage and my mother being of Irish/Dutch (American) heritage were not allowed to marry in California due to California's anti-miscegenation law which did not allow inter-racial marriages between Filipinos and Caucasian women. This resulted in my parents having to travel to Lordsburg, New Mexico to obtain a marriage license, be married there by a justice of the peace and then return to Stockton, California for a church wedding. In a book written by one of my first cousins who herself is of a Filipino and Mexican mixture mentions that her mother and father also had to leave the state to be married due to California's anti-miscegenation law. (See Family Wedding photos "Where it all Started" on the adjacent pages)

Alfonso Agdeppa Fillon and Mary Ellen Kirkpatrick 1945
Parents

Parents Wedding Party 1945 Stockton California
Left to Right Victor Castro - Friend and Relative, Bro. Asuncion, Asst. Pastor, Rev Alex Ancheta D.D.,
Alfonso Fillon (Groom) Rev. Hornize, Rev. Julian Bernabe, Founding Filipino Assembly of the First Born,
Ruth Farber - Mother's Friend, Singer and Organist, Friend - Carmen Asuncion, Life-long Friend
Patricia Ancheta. Front Noni Farber - Daughter of Ruth Farber, Seated Mary Kirkpatrick Fillon - Bride

The fact that my parents were not allowed a marriage license in the city and state where I was born. Thus, legitimacy or American illegitimacy had an impact upon me and how I viewed myself and situations repetitively throughout my life. The main impact of this issue on me was the fact that it planted a psychological seed of being socially illegitimate and thus I felt shades of being "illegitimate" all my life. Sometimes more directly, sometimes only subliminally but nonetheless it left a negative cloud hanging over my head. It had an impact my on perception of my self-worth and lifelong inter-racial relationships. Noteworthy about the miscegenation laws passed during that period of time was the fact that the laws got progressively more restrictive as time went on until the law was declared unconstitutional by Calif. Supreme Court and then only by a slim margin. At the federal level, the unconstitutionality was not acted on until a 1967 in Loving v Virginia:

- Anti-Miscegenation laws existed in California from 1850 progressively adding Mongolians, Japanese, Malays; inclusive language in 1945;

- Anti-Miscegenation law was not repealed by the conscience of lawmakers in California until 1948 in Perez v Sharp -narrowly ruled unconstitutional by vote of -4 to 3
- 1967 U. S. Supreme Court ruling of unconstitutionality 9-0 in Loving v Virginia

I had actually wondered if I had a valid point of view about the psychological damage to my outlook on my value as a person and macro elements of self-concept caused by the affectations of the miscegenation law. Shortly after a recent presentation I made in my local community about recent presentation on this subject, experiences of a Filipino/ Caucasian mestizo, I was approached by a mestizo professor and several other members at the audience who shared with me that they too had felt this way (questions of self-worth based on the concepts of anti-miscegenation law) but had not had an opportunity or inclination to express it. The consensus of participants was that each mestizo had felt that uncomfortable feelings I talk about throughout life as recipients of some form of subtle discrimination and rejection but had wondered if they were being overly sensitive, or if the discrimination expressing such feelings were even valid and normal. That feeling of uneasiness and turbulence I understand. The description for me, having been the recipient of racism throughout my early life and sporadically in my adult life is that it is almost as though there was a raging river within me seeking to break out of the confining banks containing it and look for the peace and calm of a glassy ocean. With age, financial comfort, conquered life experiences and chosen social environments, some elements of the smooth glassy surface of a calm ocean reflecting the moon light is now reality for me, for the most part.

I recollect that as a youth about ten years of age I left home late one evening running off to my aunt's home for refuge. On the surface, I do not now remember why I ran off, but I think it had to do something with one parental disapproval conflict compounded by pressures of the raging river syndrome as mentioned above. The next and last time I ran off was after high school and had to do with irresolvable parental disapproval of a nice girl I was dating. I wanted to have personal control over personal decisions in my life and felt it was time to move on. Thank God for the local YMCA. I am very disappointed when I drive by there at this age for the building is completely shuttered and closed. I think what a support and refuge it was for young men like myself; those like me for whom it might be a refuge for but that it is no longer available.

More modern behavioral studies have concluded that such broad exposure of an individual to negative attitudes, labels, words, invalidations and similar projections do have a tremendous impact on the psyche and behavior of individuals so exposed. Lawful discrimination is an experience that I never got over the impact of. Discrimination related to my brown side or the hostile verbalizations directed at me during my childhood, youth and adulthood periodically from and by members of the white (American) community lingers. It is always there tending to raise it's ugly head in those quiet times of loneliness, quiet and tranquility and remind me that no matter how much I have accomplished, I will never be of the majority race or of common acceptance. Such is the effect of bias and racism in America.

To underscore this conclusion is the fact that the Caucasian side of my family, my mother's side has generally not reached out to me, to befriend me or make me feel welcomed of their own accord. As unfortunate as this may be for me, I have grown quite content to respect their discomfort with their association with a relative with a brown skin and their seeming contentment with keeping their distance. As I reflect back, I remember my mother and I taking the train back to Illinois top visit family when I was about five or six years of age and meeting my grandmother who lived upstairs at my aunt's house. During the whole time there about two weeks, my grandmother of European descent never hugged me once or touched me nor did my aunt. My mother and aunt explained this away as my grandmother being "legally blind". This now causes me an – "lol" (laughing out loud in e-mail language) now as I think about it. Looking back, I can only imagine that my mother's side of the family must have really held my brownness, even at that early age, as really bad; like "leper" bad and likely contagious. So when "locals" shouted racial insults at me, it seemed to have a double negative impact on me and my already damaged psyche. After all, if your own relatives shy away from you – your brownness as a mestizo must be seen as really despicable, akin to being "bound for hell" as a good old Baptist preacher might say at a Sunday service of the past.

Author in middle at 18 back from Boot Camp 175 lbs. slim and trim with Mother left, and father on right.

Fond Boyhood memories of Mom, Dad and Downtown Filipino Culture

Growing up in Stockton I found an unspoken pressure to stay within expected boundaries, to know "my place" least I be singled out for ridicule, harsh words or even demeaning or insults, ethnic or references to animal likenesses. I therefore steered clear of predominantly white areas of the city and white business environments and dry goods stores without my white mother who might draw stares of curiosity but no comments. I did enjoy our shopping visits to Sears – Roebucks and Montgomery Ward's stores that were known for a plethora of merchandise from clothing to appliances and all kinds of sports equipment. Even a visit to Centro-Mart, a large oriental run grocery store was a delight to visit for me.

At the time, many Filipinos congregated along the southern end of El Dorado street just south and north of Lafayette Street and South of Washington Street. Given the legendary history of wide-scale attacks and beating of Filipinos in agricultural labor centers in California, I concluded that there was safety in numbers and that congregating here was both a safety net and social center. I remember the odor of "smelly" cigars but I never thought to as my father's cousin but referred to by me as "Uncle" who frequented the area just exactly what they were; some referred to them as "Toscano's or Toscanys" (a highly fermented cigar from Toscany, Italy). In any case, when I went to pick up Chinese food I could often find a distant relative or friend of my fathers braced on a parking meter "holding court'" Years later while in high school, I would frequent the area after school for a friendly game of pool with my Filipino mestizo friends. I appreciated the times there, the culture and being around groups of "Manongs" (Senior Filipinos). Returning to Stockton I personally am suspicious of motives of "City Fathers" or "whomever" that decided to run a freeway through the middle of "Filipino Town" as I called it. In doing so it also shadowed the downtown senior center where, when coming through town to visit or on business, I could find my mother having lunch, visiting her caseworker or just visiting her friends.

As a little boy, my father, mother and I would park the car facing west on Washington Street just East of El Dorado. Once there, father would purchase bituka (sautéed pig belly sautéed in soy sauce and some kind of wine) displayed in the store window; mom would purchase Chinese fortune cookie and I would get the benefit of what I considered a tasty treat of bituka and get to opine optimistic good fortunes read from the little paper fortunes from the fortune cookies. On occasion there was a special treat when we would go up the stairs over the "bituka" store to a Chinese restaurant or across the street to the other. Memory fails me at the moment so forgive me, but I believe one restaurant was Canton Low, the other On Lock Sam's, the other Gan Chy around the corner. On other occasions, there were after church dinners at the El Dorado

Chinese restaurant south of town across from McKinley Park; there I would have my favorite, "pork noodles".

Perceptions and Assumptions and Mental Processing – Walk Down Memory Lane

Listening to my parents mull over and recount the experiences and encounters they had in trying to get married as a mixed race couple in the United States and particularly in Stockton California caused me to realize that there was a racial inequality in our society where I was concerned and - that this inequity was based on my ethnic composition. It caused me to realize that racial inequality was a matter of fact and that I would always be up against this element throughout my life. These accepted societal *mores* drew into question the legitimacy of me as a person in my community, state and nation in my consciousness and psyche. During coffee table discussions between my mother and father, dad and mom on occasion reflected on harassment they received at a Lordsburg New Mexico restaurant from a Caucasian male due to being a mixed-race couple and the fact that this Caucasian male did not see this as "right". I conclude this was another anti-miscegenation advocate.

I realized that this bias was not only reflective of the feelings of individuals whom I would also encounter throughout life in America with "feelings" about me as a Brown American, but that it was also sanctioned, legitimized and enforced by American law makers and by statutory law and this reality would haunt me in some way, shape or form throughout my life.

- My reality at the time based on existing laws by law makers left me no other choice but to conclude that racial bias was real and a foundation of the America my father left his native country for to migrate to America to live the "American Dream".
- Born in American and thus an American Citizen, I took solace and faith in the fact that this is what my father wanted for his family and I should then accept the concept of discrimination as

a reality of life for brown people, particularly Filipino mestizos as in my case, attempt to minimize its impact on my life and work hard to succeed in spite of it.

Looking back and examining my father's reaction to some situations and encounters with Caucasians, I can now see why sometimes his interactions and reactions involving Caucasian strangers seemed more of an overreaction given the context of the encounter. This caused me to be even more cautionary to inter-racial encounters. On occasion, my own reaction to similar situations seemed to have no rational basis. I simply reacted as I did because I had seen my father offended by similar condescending behavior.

As I look back to the innocence of my youth and my childhood, I remember times when I was feeling hurt by harsh discriminatory words, labels and /or experiences when I would look at my mother with her fair, white skin, blond hair and blue eyes and envy that fact that she was of the Caucasian race and that "brownness" was not a battle she would ever have to fight or feel. I left home after high school however during that time I perceived that my mother's battle was that of a blond, blue-eyed lady being married to or in company of a brown skinned man – a Filipino. On the flip side it was an existence I was destined to never experience – that of having a "white" side; I would have to put up with the harshness of discrimination with no avenue of escape for all of my life.

My Perspective and Experience on Bias.

My mother was purported to be of Irish, German and Dutch heritage. We are all aware of the ability to trace heritages via computerized research. However, as of this time I have chosen to rely on word of mouth from mother and personal recollections, correct or incorrect, for the sake of allowing word of mouth to be the racial concept from which I write. Mother was raised in southern Illinois and therefore knowledgeable of southern type discrimination in practice. Mother could and did occasionally articulate the racial biases of the population from which she originated and from which she migrated. I had heard from other southerners unverified stories of "Negroes" not making it out of town before dark and being observed the next morning having been hung. I would not have wanted to chance being a Mestizo – Filipino Caucasian in those areas of "zero" tolerance in those communities and in those times. Based on what mother knew of discriminatory attitudes based on mixed skin color, she made every effort to shelter and protect me from exposure to such biases. She tried to facilitate possible ways for me to live as happily as possible in spite of biases and to not feel the pain of such projected and direct discrimination and/or discriminatory practices and actions by "Americans" in our community as they were referred to. It was as if, at first glance, I was not an "American".

Unfortunately, that protection and protective umbrella of my mother's efforts only worked at home. When I left the shelter of my home, I became exposed to the real, frequent and often blatant biases of others; predominantly those from "Americans" of the Caucasian race. I was quite aware that she understood racial bias, having been raised in it in southern Illinois, and that some assimilating of it in her formative years and culture was natural.

I assumed however, that my mother marrying a brown person, a Filipino, meant that deep personal prejudice was not inherent in her outlook toward others and "real" exceptions could be made for me by enough "whites" in my life to matter. I also hoped that these exceptions would be enough to positively matter in me achieving my share of the American dream for which my father left his original home thousands of miles behind to realize. Within my heart and soul, I truly did hope that there would be "whites" who would make similar exceptions for me despite my skin color and mixed race; that they would sincerely accept me. Clearly understanding mom's need to protect me from biases was a dilemma for me.

As a young boy, for instance and in an effort to both sensitize me to bias and mitigate prejudice due to skin color, mom suggested that I not play in the sun and to cover my skin and wear a hat when in the sun. She suggested that I do this in order to minimize the tanning of my skin and thus attempt to blunt blatant prejudice from the Caucasian American population. Through this I concluded that being of a darker color must not be a good thing and that by being darker, I was likely to face whatever bias might be projected onto one of darker color by members of the Caucasian population. In a subtle way, such pronunciations from my mother even tended to lend to the credibility of "color" prejudice and that in some small ways, perhaps subliminally, such biases were justified.

There are a number of ways to look at this from my perspective and I ask myself:

— Was it protectiveness or defensiveness on mom's part?
— Was it a genuine concern for me based on society at the time – Reference the anti-miscegenation law, that would be a real basis of concern for me at some time in my life due to skin color and my racial composition.

In this context I chose to imagine that my mother loved me and did not want to see me vulnerable to the pain she knew I would be exposed to. She had seen it first hand in her church organization, in the community, and as a partner in a bi-racial marital relationship. In truth, as a person of mixed Filipino-Caucasian composition with brown skin, I was in essence, doomed to community discrimination. As such I could not be light skinned enough, blue-eyed enough or blond enough to effectively mitigate community standards or foundations of discrimination.

I am glad that my father evolved into a religious man and was able to apply biblical scripture and teachings of tolerance to those individual circumstances of prejudice and related hostilities he suffered at the hands of some white males and females who harbored prejudice against the Filipino immigrant. The best scenario my father could hope for from such biased people was in the context of the projectors of discrimination and mental or verbal hostilities was that he, the Filipino immigrant, was a "necessary evil". What I could hope for was the tolerance extended me as his "little brown bastard" child as I found myself occasionally referred to in the city of streets of Stockton as I wandered the streets shopping or performing errands for the family and I might do something that would stir the ire of a white American. In the Viet Nam War, pg. 359, Ward and Burns, Knopf, New York 2017, Gen. Julian Ewell is quoted as rallying troops of the Ninth Infantry in three delta provinces of Viet Nam (circa 1969) to kill "four thousand of *these little bastards* a month". So, it is likely that the term "little bastards" was a common American idiom for referring to people who fit their perception of "Asian looking" physical characteristics. I am not an authority in this area so I will leave it to the scholarly to refute my assertion.

As I matured, I came to understand that dad and the Filipino immigrants were important to the bottom line of farmers and business owners as laborers in crop harvesting and behind the scenes in the service industry(s). I did eventually come to appreciate the American farmers for it was they who out of necessity, offered the Filipino immigrant work and therefore income opportunities vital to survival. I realized that, though not enough to break the chains of subservient indenture, it was up to each individual to break their individual chains. Some were able to break free and become independent, many of that generation were not.

Dad had worked "the fields" and in various agricultural settings. I almost used the term "positions" as I referred to Dad's working in the various agricultural settings. Then I thought "how Americanized, educated and above all 'distant" I have become from the reality of my upbringing where the people we associated with had "jobs" not the loftiness implied by the term "position". These settings dad worked in were harvesting fruits and vegetables in his young life during and after his successful migration to his beloved United States. During the war, he supplemented his income from any steady job he might have by working in the fields of California agriculture. I have vivid memories of playing with tinker-toys on a "lug" or wooden box for filling fruit while my parents moved from row to row harvesting tomatoes. Now as an adult, I lament the fact that my parents – especially my mother - were relegated to economic survival in such an arduous way but times were tough for most everyone at that time; my parents did what they had to do – I never heard either of them complain. If anything, there was a benefit and that was a closeness each shared in that my mother had chosen this life also. Such poverty had a tremendous effect on my psyche the rest of my life but most profoundly affected my self-esteem during my childhood, pre-adolescence and post-adolescence. Its impact was like the weight of railroad boxcar resting on your shoulders. First, feeling illegitimate due to the illegality of my parent's inter-racial marriage – even against the law, overt discrimination experienced for being brown skinned, being on the bottom of the socio-economic scale (even poor), and the overall impact of limited to no social standing the community. As a post-adolescent I vowed to never be subservient, without material wealth or lacking in professional and financial accomplishment. Mom was designated to stay at home, raise me and manage the household which she did very well.

In my family, breaking such chains of economic mediocrity and lower social and financial status elements were fostered onto the shoulders of the next succeeding firstborn generation and thus fell squarely upon my shoulders. I eventually broke the psychological and economic bondage of being a first-generation Mestizo Filipino in America, over time, given my educational, professional status achievement and some financial acumen compared to, but did so happily, in honor of - my father and mother.

In retrospect, I feel I was seduced by the comforts of the American mid-level societal norms I had achieved. That being "a little better off" was comforting; I was lulled into satisfaction and complacency. Along the way, I lost some of the passion to be "extremely" successful. Because I became marginally successful in the career field which I was in, I came to feel that I was actually one of and a part of – "the system"! A real American! Discrimination seemed non-evident in an individual sense. Growing up I had not seen the tangible evidence my father had seen posted on signs stating "Positively No Dogs or Filipinos" and therefore I succumbed to going along with the program. In fact, however, discrimination against the Filipino-Caucasian Mestizo was every bit in existence and every bit as deadly. The perpetrators were to change form and method, even color. This is a story that needs to be uncovered and those perpetrators need to be identified in some way, shape and form and held accountable in another writing.

As a matter of course, during the period of which I speak, there were some Filipinos who were educated and in the professions. Some (a few) I have spoken to in this category did not admit to experiencing discrimination, professional or otherwise. To this, their view of denial, I am somewhat skeptical but accepting of their purported reality of "equality". It then is no wonder, in my mind that Filipino "protective orders" or lodges as they were referred to as when I was young, were seemingly more in the nature of a "social order' than a civil rights advocacy group with commensurate mission. My father's cousin was referred to as a "Grand Master" and I did not know what that meant or related to; in my youth, that term and it's inference felt ominous. I do know that the family had a big house and two Cadillacs. I did not know what those material symbols equated to, and still don't. As I wasn't familiar with that life-style I did not even ask questions about it and family did not talk about it in front of me.

For those who seemingly did not experience discrimination, I am happy for them. This happiness for them in no way means I fully accept their view or their verbalization that they were not discriminated against. I feel it more likely that because they may have tended to associate with professionals or the upper or educated middle economic "American", prejudice (not discrimination) was not so obvious and in those circles, more carefully veiled and skillfully concealed. I could conclude two other things: one was that in their mind, no matter what the White man did or said, the white American was the "superior" and was not to be questioned; the other was that it just did not matter to them; especially if the recipient Filipino was getting what he or she wanted out of the encounter. If so, why not just fly under the radar and avoid being "outed". Another possible alternative which suits me, though not exactly very kind, is the conclusion that the recipient of the discrimination simply was not fully equipped to feel it or recognize it, for whatever reason. Given the reality of my world as a first generation Filipino-Caucasian American youth, I operated under the same and similar premise and parallel of the proverbial question of the 1960's: If a tree falls in the forest and no one is around to hear it fall, does it make a sound? I guess it would depend on some definitions. Similarly, if a decision was to be made about you by Caucasian Americans; did prejudice ever enter into the decision about you? My conclusion has usually been, absent evidence to the contrary, "it is most likely that some element of prejudice was present in the decision-making process. Given my exposure to decision making processes in American bureaucracies, I feel discrimination against the Filipino-Caucasian mestizo was likely a factor, and prejudice and bias still does exist!". There are exceptions, honest exceptions! Those individuals I have encountered that were strong enough, or ethical enough, to stand on their own two feet and support you or me, the Filipino-Caucasian mestizo, I hold as rare and possessing an ethical quality worthy of the highest honor and respect. I further feel that such an unbiased, objective person in-turn, deserving of my support and the ultimate allegiance. I was raised to believed that the loyalty of a Filipino was akin to none other. In my experience I feel because of such principled upbringing, I may have on occasion been loyal to a fault.

Author: Al Fillon in Happier Times, Going Native in the Islands

Hawaiian Paradise - But Not for the Filipino Cane Field Workers of the 1920's

I have always enjoyed vacations in Hawaii and likened the islands, the culture and environment, the closest one could come to paradise on earth (except when I was driving a rental car and had my rear window bashed in - likely due to the rental agency sticker on it)

Dad referred to and talked about working in the cane fields of Hawaii before his final journey to mainland California, USA. I, unfortunately was too young to know a much about my father's experience working in Hawaii but it was evident to me that dad had spent a sufficient amount of time working there and assimilating into the Hawaiian culture, customs and ways of life. Further, I did not even understand why he spent time there or the circumstance by which he left there to arrive at his final migratory goal, the United States until later in my life. It was during the late 1920 and there was a lot of labor conflict in the Hawaiian Island involving Filipino sugar cane field labor which consisted mainly of Filipinos. Over time growing up I gathered from dads occasional lamenting that dad looked upon the Hawaiian culture and experiences fondly. However, I also got the impression that regardless of the aggressive prejudice dad experienced in America, labor was comparatively more predictable here in America compared to his experience in Hawaii. It was later in my life as a young man on vacation when I toured the pineapple and cane fields of Hawaii, that I came to question the beauty of cane fields for the Filipinos that ended up working in them. While the other tourist were "oohing" and "awing" information shared with them by tour guides, and sipping pineapple juice, that I reflected back to the struggles and tough times Filipinos experienced as migrant workers on the beautiful Islands of Hawaii. In retrospect, aside from my father's skills with the Hawaiian steel guitar, I believe his penchant for most Country Music was related to the twang of the Country slack steel guitar back up for country singers.

Upon arrival in California, dad continued working in agriculture until his conversion to the protestant religion and acceptance in a bible college at Glad Tidings Bible Institute on Ellis Street in San Francisco, California. Dad completed the four years of Bible school there. I was surprised how many Filipinos attended school with other white student both male and female living in dorms. Dad hoped to become a minister as did his brother. However, though dad was not able to apply such training to support a family, a great number of Christian values, teachings and practices permeated my home and upbringing. Christian practices of the time of my upbringing were very stringent. I was not allowed to attend movies, dances or participate in other social situations outside of church and home. Church was a blessing for there were other youth there, Mestizos like myself as well as mestizos of the Filipino Mexican mixture some of which were distant relatives. Essentially however, it is my feeling that my social interaction and sophistication was more limited than that for other youth of my age.

Mother had unshakeable hopes that I would become a minister in life. I am told by friends that her prayers were always in that same vein that I would see a calling to the ministry. Unfortunately, I had watched my father attempt that endeavor and was aware of the tremendous hopes he had of successfully becoming a minister; the amount of time, study, schooling and devotion he had put in in pursuit of that goal. Unfortunately, I was aware of the bias and prejudice in the religious field and in the organization in which he and my mother had attained ministerial licenses. As a youthful, stand in "deacon" assistant devoted church goer, I did not see enough "green" (money) of sizeable numerical denominations in the offering plate, nor was I exposed to organized religious leader compensation packages, even at the larger churches. Although I did feel the calling was a noble one, I unfortunately, did not feel myself to be "called" on by the spirit and at seventeen years of age I joined the military. While in the service, I was happy to attend church on Sundays wherever I was in the world, most of the time in Asia and Viet Nam.

Eventually in life, I attended a religious conference with a friend who was a minister of the Baptist denomination. After some discussion and soul searching, I became an ordained minister. Unfortunately, by that time, my mother had passed away. It is also ironic that later, on the one Sunday I was able to make it back to my home church after returning to Stockton, that a visiting pastor was giving a sermon on Moses wandering in the desert for 40 years. Another irony was that, as I meditated during the sermon, I realized that it had been 40 years that I had been away from what I considered my home church.

Dad eventually found civil service employment with the local school district, made a comfortable living for his family and retired happy with his level of achievement. I did not particularly accept that dad could not have accomplished more professionally than he did. However, he was comfortable with what he had accomplished all things considered. In retrospect I can reflect, share and understand his feelings. On one occasion I heard my father share that his abilities in the workforce were "limited". It was because of that innuendo on his part that I made up my mind to strive to be successful though I did not have a plan. I did not have a "success coach" and did not get the level of counseling, particularly "guidance" that I needed to go to college. Luckily, my high school associates talked about it and I became sensitized to it. My eventual plan was real estate investment which brought some success. I was psychologically setback in this goal in some respects however, by the harsh economic experiences of my mother and father during my upbringing. When I invested in a duplex in Stockton, my parents said "Son be very careful.". When I bought ten units in southern California, I was again haunted by their ingrained cautionary fears. Once again, I heard, "Son, be very careful.". While I was confident in the figures and experienced in flipping properties, the cautions of my parents always hung there over my head causing a little seed of self-doubt I would have been better off without. Once again, in retrospect, I believe that being a first generation Filipino - Caucasian American, and having been victim of racist labels and orientation, that scenario acted like a chain of reservation around his and my ankle plays a huge part in my father's caution on financial matters.

Looking back and examining my father's reaction to some situations and encounters with Caucasians, I can now see why sometimes his interactions and reactions involving Caucasian strangers seemed more of an overreaction given the context of the encounter. This caused me to be even more cautionary to inter-racial encounters. On occasion, my own reaction to similar situations seemed to have no rational basis. I simply reacted as negatively as I did because I had seen my father offended by similar condescending behavior. Given the current socio-political world and how my racial assimilation process fits in, I find I am less emotionally sensitive and less suspicious. Maybe less suspiciousness as to racial motive makes me less sensitive and consequently, less vulnerable. But again, I feel that financial success as well as personal and educational achievement have played a significant part in mitigating my feelings of vulnerability and personal susceptibility to inevitable biases and prejudices.

Reacting to Racial Bias, Discrimination; Recognizing my own Biases and Living with it.

Based on my own experience in my local community as a child and over time I concluded that bias and prejudice was a reality in America, not only as a matter of law, but as a social reality, to be expected from Caucasian Americans. I was always cognizant of the aura of mass hunt downs and beating of Filipinos in Watsonville, California and other tales about Filipino vulnerability to racism and felt that such aggressions could legally happen to me at any time. Given the severity of discomfort and deep pain I felt as a recipient of prejudice but particularly discrimination, I chose not to overlook this element of reality and felt I was always the better for it.

In my personal life I found that social and professional conclusions about the minority but in my case, that of a Filipino-Caucasian American, my attitude, opinion, professional ability, performance, knowledge aptitude, experience and the like has usually been suspect when a Caucasian, male or female is involved in evaluating me and passing judgement on my knowledge or ability. I can validate that feeling because, as a top-level manager in my profession, there are many times when I have seen and heard the reservations expressed about minorities and Asians articulated. It so happens that friends and associates have shared bits and pieces of conversations in decisions about me, after the fact, and on a social level. Thank goodness for sometimes being known by the right people, at the right time. There is something to be taken serious about the American saying: "it's not what you know, but who you know!". You can take that tidbit to the bank - so true! I am fortunate in that, as stated earlier, I had the foresight to prepare for this stigma of bias by taking advantage of all opportunities available to me to add professional credentials and certifications, self-improvement experience forums - formal and informal, to my personal and professional tool bag. Luckily for me, I have had the opportunity to address many challenges and thus self-actualize success. By meeting those challenges in many different settings eventhough some were uncomfortable, I have been able to use them to increase self-confidence, and reaffirm my competence; at least in my own mind if not in the mind of others. I ask myself and the reader may also ask of me, why is all this reaffirmation and self-improvement validation important - Americans don't have these problems (though we know they do have their own doubts and failings). However, I know that this is just another psychological deficit hurdle of which the seed was planted long ago; I was born into it. Its basis goes back to having been born into, first, a frowned upon and unlawful parental unison by virtue of the anti-miscegenation law, and secondly, being born with the brown skin of my migrant father and therefore doomed to be a life-long recipient of bias and racial prejudice.

During the early part of my career, I asked myself why do I have to go over this unpleasant experience of being perceived as inadequate and thus, me, needing to prove myself over and over again throughout my career when others did not? At first, I thought it was because I was not quite "professional". But I then realized after analysis, that even if I were a renowned heart surgeon, there would still be the same doubts about me due to my ethnicity and being a brown Filipino-Caucasian American. I later concluded that this type of doubt and prejudice was a matter of assimilated or learned behavior and reinforced from one generation to another; further reinforced by the social circle of the individuals involved. I further concluded that biases are reflective of the exposure, experience and descriptive adjectives; positive or negative definitions, articulated from those around the perpetrators starting at an early age. I concluded that discriminatory behavior and related negative verbal epithets I was exposed to, were a matter of internal influence and family programming; also, a matter of personal choice as to whether or not one chose to relate to another person or people based on that biased point of view.

In my own case, I could have futilely chosen to affiliate with my mother's ethnicity and color or race or my father's color and/or race. In coming to a decision on which ethnicity I favored, I took into consideration that based on my mother's inflections that I should be careful not to get darker and protect myself from tanning while playing, I would be faced with an undaunting task. In reality, I was already brown and not "browning" any further was not likely to make much of a difference in being accepted by "Americans".

Thus, I chose to mentally embrace and affiliate with the brown side of my mixture. In this safe harbor I did not have to explain, defend or attempt to force association; I only had to learn to live with it. It is a shame that at such an early age I even had to make such a choice. Fortunately, despite my mother's clarity on what I must overcome in terms of racial bias and prejudice, she encouraged me to see myself as being as "white" as I was "brown". For that perspective bestowed on me by my mother, I am in retrospect, truly grateful. I do notice that most of my male friends who are the same type mestizo as I (Filipino-Caucasian) had similar leanings toward accepting that they would be assumed brown and treated as such overlooking the "white" ethnic component of their makeup.

My First Hand Exposure to "Southern Brand" Racial Segregation in Practice

My first-hand exposure to an actual racial "Jim Crow" segregation encounter and related aggressive treatment had to do with a Black youth boarding a bus in Alton, Illinois when I was about six years of age. The

Black youth attempted to sit in the middle of the bus and the bus driver immediately addressed the young man by vacating his bus driver's seat and approaching the youth with an admonishment that he was to sit in the back of the bus. I was too young to understand what was going on and being from California, was not exposed to the routine of the practice in Alton. My mother explained what had happened and from that I wondered, if I were older, and not escorted by my mother, might I have faced the same fate? This experience made me very uncomfortable and the matter remains unsolved in my mind and psyche to this day. If I were to ask the question as to application, I expect I would get an answer today, that no, I wouldn't have been treated the same way. However, if I were to go back in time and board the bus, I expect that I would have been treated similar to how that youth was treated. The dilemma, come in that, not being familiar with the "Jim Crow" practices, I would not have known why I was being told to go to the back of the bus at the time and may have faced a very serious, unpleasant outcome. My mother tried to minimize any reflections on me related to this experience.

I do note that while in Illinois, on a visit with my mother to her home town and family and visiting a married couple friends of my mother, I was physically abused by an older white man. The man thought it was funny to rub his whiskers over my cheeks causing me pain and then soothe my reddened face with rubbing alcohol. I was too young to understand the significance of this act at the time, or even the basis for it; or his enjoyment in doing it. Now, in retrospect I regard him as just another sick American out to harm a "brown-skinned, little brown-bastard, child. A psychologist could probably add a deviant label of some kind to this. His wife, incidentally, seemed to think nothing of it.

Another situation comes to mind as I watched the child of a Caucasian family my mother was visiting, collect a box of black kittens and repeatedly toss the kittens from the porch into the street and retrieve them and toss them again. I always wondered if he was doing that because the kittens were black in color or, was he trying to make some kind of point to me? The child, about my age, finally quit the "kitten toss" when his mother called his name and said, "okay, one more time, and that's enough for today". Wow!

Know Where You Don't Belong - Especially in Southern Cultures

In retrospect, it might have been better if my mother would have had a candid conversation with me about racial differences, biases and prejudices; at least to the level that a six-year old child might understand. But, how does a Caucasian mother tell her child, "in the eyes of some white people, you are not as good or acceptable - be careful". I believe, and accept, that such articulation might have been too much for even my mother to mentally and emotionally confront. In the animal kingdom, I have been told that in some wild kingdom species, a mother will sacrifice the least perfect offspring so the more vibrant of the group survive. Luckily, my mother did not have to confront sacrificing me as such a less perfect conforming offspring to "American" standards of that time. I reflect on this as I recall a situation in which, while on our trip to visit my mother's roots, my mother went to visit her sister in a little town, Roxana, Illinois. The residence was a large white palatial home on a very large estate size corner lot: my aunt married well into the Oklahoma, oil business. My only cousin there was of the dating age, about sixteen years old and was put in charge of me. I remember being allowed to play with a ball by myself in the large back yard. However, being alone, I strayed around to the front yard where my cousin was visiting with her boyfriend outside of a car in the driveway. I approached my cousin and her suitor. I could tell by my cousin's surprise and her shouting directions to "Go to the back yard!" that I, the "monkey was out of the barrel or the black sheep". Even at that early age, I concluded that she was very embarrassed by my appearance and I wondered why her demeanor had changed so uncharacteristically. From the expressions, now, I can imagine that as another "little brown bastard" situation. Later, I remember my aunt, out of earshot of my mother, chastising me for being a "bad boy" and being where I shouldn't have been or "belong". Another situation involving the "little brown bastard" syndrome different context or as they would often say in the military, "same old shit, different day".

Another situation comes to mind while I was visiting in the South. While visiting another family, I watched the child of a Caucasian family my mother was visiting, collect a box of black kittens and repeatedly toss the kittens from the porch into the street; retrieve them and toss them again. I always wondered if he was doing that because the kittens were black in color or, was he trying to make some kind of point to me? The child, about my age, finally quit the "kitten toss" when his mother called his name and said, "okay, one more time and that enough for today". Wow!

Per my father, his perspective as a pre-arrival to the United States was the pressing desire to become an American and try to take advantage of opportunities and the purported American benevolent way of life. It seems that in that day and time for the Filipino and perhaps many other ethnic immigrants, becoming an American was a first and foremost burning desire and that each immigrant would be able to be accepted into the American landscape as an equal. I believe, based on exposure to many other Filipino relatives and Filipinos I have spoken to of that generation that – this was their desire also. I shudder when I think that my father and most other Filipinos certainly did not realize the degree of prejudice they would experience in the United States in the process of reaching out for this dream. I was dismayed by the stories about experiences I heard of *bullying* of Filipinos by "Americans" as the "Caucasians" were referred to at the time. Part of the allure of the United States and the aura of being an American was sewn in the Philippine Islands by Americans who served there in the military and in other official posts in World War I and World War II like American Army General Douglas Macarthur. Per records and documentation, Filipinos found the Americans whom they worked for, observed and even associated with, to be a kind, warm and benevolent. The fact that Americans were willing to be in the Philippines during the war fighting a brutal and potentially conquering and over-whelming force of Japanese and fight side by side with Filipinos, I conclude, gave the

Filipino people the feeling that "Americans" were friends; that these Americans saw them as people worth fighting for. It led them to believe that the Filipino in the eyes of the American was worthwhile – even an equal in theirs and God's eyes. One of my uncles in the Philippines involved in the Bataan death march was said to feel this way. Little did the Filipinos know however, that once they got to America, they would be referred to as "monkeys", "heathens" and "out to steal white women". Little did those Filipinos know that in Stockton, California and other cities in the United States or "America" as Filipinos so lovingly referred to it as, that almost simultaneously, there were signs posted in hotels to the equivalent of "No Dogs or Filipinos Allowed". Mom referring to the signage prohibiting Filipinos, found it repugnant. Filipino mestizo children, as I personally experienced, would be referred to without reservation, as" little brown bastards" or "monkeys" in the streets of my "American" community by American men and women of that era as was widely witnessed and also documented in literature on the Filipino experience.

In retrospect, I find it noteworthy that my father shared experiences of ethnic bias as they came to mind or were experienced, but did not highlight the fact that these experiences were based on prejudice or more correctly racial/color bias. I now believe that he did not highlight those conclusions in my presence hoping that he would not emphasize those realities and imprint them in my psyche. While he tried to protect me from that reality, he hoped I would be able to minimize those experiences in my own life and would more aptly regard myself as socially equal and unquestionably a real American to the extent possible.

As a child, I was fortunate to attend Stockton southside schools that had a mixture of different cultures, ethnicities and socio-economic diversities. Thus, ethnicity difference issues were not a predominant factor to deal with in the school environment day in and day out. However, there were the clusters of Caucasian student groups that would verbalize ethnic insults as a first response to conflicts and or disagreements on the playground. The school ground and classmates were a great avenue and setting for me to assimilate into the American culture in. The schools I attended were integrated both racially and economically to some degree. Few students seemed to have more financial advantage than any other and there were minimal language barriers. I do not think I would have been pleased to have to attend school with students "bussed in" who were financially affluent evidenced by attitude or dress or who additionally exhibited enhanced arrogance in verbal conversations or cultural attitudes. I still wonder about the real reason for bussing poor students to affluent neighborhood schools and contributing to the experiences of feeling further demeaned or affluent children to poor neighborhoods where the feeling of misunderstanding and deprecating attitudes are at play, absent maturity and conflict resolution skills.

I was very comfortable in the educational social environment I found myself in at eight years of age and in the third grade. Conflict came when I mixed with Caucasian youth from other parts of town mainly the north which consisted basically of established Caucasian families for whatever reason. The same scenario of social and environmental comfort followed in Junior high (Grades 7 through 9) and Senior High School, (Grades 10 through 12) where I continued to attended schools on the southside of the city. Given an equal mix of white, black, brown and other ethnicities I was able to attend school with a minimum of thought to racial inequality issues of the Caucasian – Filipino mestizo and get on with the basics of youthful life, learning and social issues.

As a family, my mother and father attended a "Filipino" protestant church on the south side of Stockton. This church was founded by Filipino religious followers for fellowship and religious worship of Filipinos and others willing to brush aside the element of American prejudice in doing so. In one sense it was a self-segregation of Filipinos for religious worship. My uncle founded a church in southern California under the umbrella of the organization in which the Stockton "Filipino" church was founded. I call this a de-facto segregation but in fact Filipinos were not warmly welcomed in the mainstream Caucasian churches in the city.

The Filipinos who founded the Filipino Firstborn church on Center Street just south of Washington Street in Stockton it seems, were mostly of the Illocano dialect but were welcoming of all Filipinos regardless of dialect and anyone else interested in worshiping with Filipinos; there weren't many others! I was born at St. Joseph's Hospital and the parsonage upstairs at church at 311 South Center Street, was my first home. At the time of my birth, 1946, Center Street was about as deep into *skid row* as one could be. The inner chuckle for me is that when at times in life I think I could have done better or been more successful, I tell myself: "I didn't do too bad for a boy born on Skid Row". For the founders of this church, it's formation was another example of insightful Filipino immigrant ingenuity as the church served as a forum and association based on a religious premise. As such, there could be comfortable worship, religious teaching, and a coming together of like-minded people and their families and a place for mutual personal and spiritual support. This Church has evolved over the 70 plus years from one location to another but many of my family still attend there. Eventually the church was relocated to Seventh Street in Stockton and now is located on Third Street in Stockton, California. Though many things about the churches and worship has changed over the years, I still attend service at this church whenever I am in Stockton. Needless to say, when I was growing up, I went to church a lot! If it wasn't for having to complete school homework, it seemed that there was some kind of church service almost every night of the week.

Although my father graduated from Glad Tidings Bible Institute, a four-year ministerial college on Ellis Street in San Francisco, my father was not comfortable with the level of welcome at the main protestant churches under the umbrella organization in and therefore exerted minimal effort to push an integrated ministry. For this I was thankful because I was already feeling unacceptable socially in the community and a more in your face rejection in a church setting would simply have been "over the top" for me.

Religious Environment and Evolution for this Filipino-Caucasian American

Real or imagined, my mother did not feel comfortable attending the Assemblies of God church in Stockton nor did I, even though both mother and father were licensed ministers in the organization. Filipinos and other minorities with "less than white or of dark skin were not unconditionally welcomed according to my mother. When I attended, I felt I stood out like a sore thumb. Therefore, I was always happier and less stressed when I attended services at the "Filipino" church. Though there was a multi-ethnic congregation it was a place where there were people like me and I felt no personal, racial, psychological or color/race hurdles to overcome; I could worship free from color discrimination. There were also other mestizo Filipino children there composed of various Caucasian, Mexican, Indian, Black and other racial combinations. Though founded by Filipinos, it is now politically incorrect to refer to it any longer as a "Filipino church" and all ethnics can and should belong. Referring to it as "international" seems more proper now. On the subject of religion, I have tried to reconcile my level of biblical Christian value belonging when I hear protestant pastors universally continue talking about Jews being the "chosen people". Not being Jewish, I work hard to accept on faith, that although I am not Jewish and a "chosen person" per the scripture, I am still okay and included in the bigger picture? Can I get an Amen? Mom wouldn't be too happy about the fact that I am still working on reconciling this dichotomy this - but am I okay with working on this challenge and that's what counts to me.

Exposure to Racial Insults and Discrimination Builds Character

I feel that the level of exposure to verbalizations of ethnic insults in school were a beneficial in some respects; a reality check for me in that there were limited numbers and from a few Caucasian students verbalizing them in my early school experience. Because such insults were limited in number, they were easier to deal with, one at a time and in a one on one basis with the perpetrator some time ending in a good fight. The personal recognition that the existence of biases verbalized in that context helped me to realize that prejudices actually existed. Sometimes confrontation would end in physical altercation. In the first grade I would cry about being teased for this and any other reason. By the second grade I began to get involved in physical fights and I was not choosy about the size of the opponent. I did not agree with the saying from teachers that, *'Sticks and stones will break my bones but names but names will never hurt me."* They, the teachers, were not the one being called dirty, nasty demeaning names and hurting inside because of it.

I enjoyed fighting and began engaging larger and larger opponents. It actually felt good to "punish" kids for their smart remarks. I think that it actually gave me an avenue and opportunity to get some of the rage and hostility out of me. Unfortunately for me I went home tired one day and fell asleep on the bed. As I lay sleeping on my back and breathing through my mouth due nasal stuffiness from a cold, my mother noticed I had a cut inner lip. I did not like suffering the third-degree and lectures mom would dish out; the interrogation went on and on. Needless to say, I decided to taper off on my aggressive behavior. It was probably a good thing that my physical aggression was finally "nipped in the bud". I found that the boys who taunted me with racial epithets would be the first to tell the teachers on me when a they a had a bloody nose, mouth or black eye; earlier, I didn't realize how easy it was to stifle the bullies regardless of their size. Still, I was trying to avoid getting into trouble however difficult it was. It also gave me time to recognize the realities of prejudice and to prepare, accept and address them throughout life in a more socially constructive way. I guess you could say that this experience did build character of some sort. I am told that in today's schools and society one is not allowed to exhibit aggressive behavior. I have mixed feelings about that. I still feel that "people' shouldn't be able to get away with regularly taunting, bullying and calling people derogatory names without paying a price for it. My mother said I should learn to control my Filipino temper and encouraged me to spend more time praying; my dad told my mother that it was the Irish in me. I thanked God that I made it through these tough times without getting into serious trouble or even hurt; that would have greatly disappointed my mother and father.

A greater level of "in your face" racial prejudice existed in other areas of Stockton, California particularly on the north side and northeast part of town; prejudices and degrading terminology were not so veiled or unspoken. More recently, relative to discrimination in the city of Stockton against Filipinos, I was approach by several Filipinos who advised me that when they were younger and attempting to buy a home in north Stockton, they were advise by real estate agents that the agents involved could not show them residential properties north of Harding Way.

Reflecting back over life some 50 years later, I am glad that I took time to reflect back on what early life was really like for me. In some ways, many in fact, I was too narrowly involved in what the world was like around me. Absent focus and clarity of thought on the matter, at times I was rather comfortable in my youthful world. I also felt that there was hope for me to succeed in life and that was the blessing of youth and innocence – maybe even ignorance.

Closing the Gap of the Mestizo - Brown Skin, White Mind

Earlier in this writing I have shared the ethnicity and physical description of my mother. The fact that when I was feeling down (not depressed) due to a recent experience of bias or racial discrimination from an encounter with other Caucasian youth or adults I would look at mom and envy her Caucasian physical features. Mom was the essence of an "American" and I envied the fact in my mind that she "belonged".

Later I was to find that the envy and respect I had for my mother was meaningful and brought a needed level of belonging and being an American – just her strength had the added benefit of quality of life, understanding and love. As I grew into manhood and after military service and for a myriad of reasons, I came to become mentally, socially and psychologically less resistive to mixing with and accepting members of the Caucasian race with less suspicion. Though as a younger person, I liked Caucasian girls as well as girls of other ethnicities; I just liked girls! Period! Conflicts had not disappeared, they just took on a different meaning and added complexities.

Adolescence Restructures Forms of Hostility and Aggression

As time passed and I tended to mature mentally and physically, I found myself less drawn into confrontive attitudes and behavior, and more drawn in to social situations and more participative in successes, and overall involvement in social situations, groups, organizations and girls where gentlemanly behavior was the expectation. I found that when interacting with girls in school and in a pseudo romantic sense, ethnicity played almost no part in relationships. For the most part girls of all ethnicities seemed to react in what could be considered girlish ways within the context of girls being girls. They liked rock n roll, dancing, recording artist, certain songs and Elvis Presley. If you had a "rock and roll jacket" which I did you were "cool"; I was cool!! I was clearly attracted to the opposite sex and social interchange. I was interested in first, femininity, sexual attractiveness (lust) and finally the sweetness of the person and their willingness to be "friends". Most readers my age can probably relate to this if they were my age at the time; about eight years or so old. I remember wishing at the time that I was a couple of years older. The "rub" here is that I simply needed to "grow into my hormones".

Starting from junior high (even sooner) I did not experience rejection from girls and raging hormones seemed to resolve whatever racial differences may have stood in the way – at least from my perspective. The difficulty for youth at this age (and for me) is that we are in a cosmos of different cultures trying to react to so many different individual expectations from the various cultures in general, rising to the new levels and roles of growth. In essence, I was finding myself a new person in a new body and trying to resolve hormonal motivators and reconcile those with evidences of physical, even psychological changes. I, and many others of my peers were lucky to make it through this period of time without any serious conflicts. From my knowledge, based on personal experiences, it is my opinion and feeling that boys at this age, do not really have a cognizant handle on what they are feeling, why they feel it or how they are going to acceptably resolve it and interact with the opposite sex. Grown women I have had this discussion with admit they also had similar anxiety and dichotomy of feelings about boys, even men at this time in their lives.

Because of the many social taboos involved in relationships and overt interactions between boys and girls at this age this is really the time for young people, likely students, to receive classes and training on interpersonal conduct and taboos; especially bridge generation children, children of immigrants new in America. We can label this experience as common to the onset of puberty; we assume that all children go through it, that it is natural, and thus all young people are prepared to go through it, properly handle the feelings and transition. It is important to assert here that from personal experience, all children are not ready to handle biological changes in their life; I was not. In today's society there are many rules, taboos, labeling and potential penalties for mistakes in acting out during this period of growth. The penalties for youthful indiscretions are too great to assume all families are sufficiently prepared at the right time in a young person's life to have the "birds and the bees" conversation.

Were the biases and prejudices from Caucasian girls still there in my life as an adolescent? I can only imagine that in a subliminal sense they were. I felt that biases did not did not go away where Caucasian girls were concerned, biases were simply temporarily suppressed. However, with hormonal factors in play, I was willing to risk rejection; didn't experience it in this context, and was the better off psychologically for having done so. I can only imagine per my experience in retrospect that convenience of daily social interaction and interpersonal friendships based on small things, like safely playing together in organized sports and other school activities, broke down barriers, at least for the moment and led to assumptions of acceptance. It was during this period of time that I found myself vulnerable to feeling "American" only to find out later that I was not American enough to fit into the Caucasian visual norm.

The dynamics here caused me to forget my indifferences to being discriminated against, at least in this social universal subset. There would be times later when once again, I would be reminded of inequality based on ethnicity, color of skin and cultural differences.

Changing my Own Paradigm on Racial Prejudice

After returning from the service and passing through the ugly experience of an unwanted divorce, there were few women around even in college, of my ethnic background Filipino-Caucasian. I subsequently encountered a very attractive blue-eyed blond. I enjoyed her soft features, smooth skin, soft purring voice, articulate conversation and company. I found her very gentle, giving, supportive and attracted to me. She was socially sophisticated and most pleasing to be with. A romantic love affair with this person provided the bridge I needed in order for me to cross over into another world that had seemed to evade and exclude me and which I had simultaneously rejected. It gave me a foundation and basis upon which to reflect and from which to better understand the feelings, culture and even emotions of my mother, her race and more American ways of life. This relationship lasted long enough and then faded without heartbreak and disappointment. Tainted by divorce and I became an equal opportunity lover intent on looking for "Ms Right", I enjoyed numerous lovers; many Caucasian. I subsequently did come to question my reality as to discrimination. Finally, and luckily, I was to develop a mutual relationship with another very attractive blue-eyed blond, married and spent many years with her.

If anything, these experiences with attractive Caucasian women helped to ameliorate feelings of discrimination I had so deeply felt as a youth and young man. I came to feel that a lot of the sting of discrimination was from within me and to continue to focus on it was a waste of time. Yes, discrimination was real and existent if not imminent.

Yet, I had been able to see it only when it was focused and imminent and directed toward me. Willie Nelson, famous Country and Western singer along with a Spanish singer, Julio Iglesias sang a song entitled "To All the Girls I've Loved Before". I reflect on that title and also appreciate my loves for their "love" and life experiences shared with me. For it is in this love and/or friendships that I found realities of life deep inside of myself and was able to right, wrong, or indifferently, mitigate racial resentment and maybe even – personal self-pity. I feel blessed to have been open and to have experienced a number of relationships involving various cultures especially Latin American. Over time, I found there is good and bad among all people, accept and enjoy the best, leave the bad behind, and don't look back.

Superiority/Inferiority Versus Identity Reality

The projection from Caucasian adults, peer students, and pre and post adolescents was that Caucasians were to be regarded as better than any/all minorities and superior in all respects without question. By virtue of exposure to racial discrimination it appeared this superiority they assumed was a "given" and we, as minorities in the community and I in particular, from a socio-political perspective in general were given to accept it as prima facie evidence. I rejected and rebelled against that notion and attitude in any way I could. Luckily, I was not overly exposed to large scale confrontive racial superiority belligerence. But innuendos and verbal abuse did take a toll on me. I mentioned earlier that I welcomed physical challenge from youthful potential combatants; an opportunity to release pent up rage and to strike back. However, as I got older, I became even less and less submissive and less accepting of a broader range of such racism and more apt to addressing it in passive aggressive ways absent punitive ramifications and reacting to racial conflict in more socially acceptable ways. As one minister and civil rights demonstrators put it at a recent civil rights demonstration, "we are just trying to get the man's knee off our neck". Well put. I found there was always someone to watch out for because as a brown skinned person", I didn't have to feel it, I just knew it could be there when I least expected it. I found in my life, that regardless of regulations and laws, racism never takes a rest, it hangs in the air. Like a chameleon, it comes in many colors, shapes and forms whether in bureaucracies, private companies or in personal associations. "On guard!" Always be vigilant and prepared was my survival motto.

Resolving Mental/Psychological Issues -Help from Unexpected Mentors

The experiences and dynamics shared in the preceding section provided a reflection in a period of time and circumstances in which I believe a foundation of attitudinal change was created from which I could put some feeling of social and racial inequity behind me. Small changes were to occur yet on the other hand, regression of disapproval was to periodically occur like an unexpected rogue wave sweeping over me and sweeping me back out to sea and psycho-social turbulence over prejudice and being white in a brown skin, a Filipino-Caucasian mestizo - a freak of nature in the white man and woman's eyes.

I owe a lot of my ability to change my own personal outlook on being the recipient of prejudice to the students of all ethnicities that I attended elementary, junior high and high school with. I owe gratitude to the various minority students of a variety of ethnic groups that I attended school with for their acceptance of me and our daily spontaneous interactions with each other. In this context the minority students accepted white members into their social and academic groups based on established interpersonal relationships likely fostered on a personal basis from their respective semi-integrated neighborhoods and vice versa. Looking back, I also appreciate the fact that the more academic oriented white students did not openly use deprecating terminology toward non-white students and me and vice versa. While I did not have many Caucasian friends, I liked and respected the ones that I did have.

I also credit as contributing factors, my encounters with two law enforcement officers. The first was a highway patrolman motorcycle officer passing through my neighborhood while I and a friend were selling "Kool Aid" from a makeshift neighborhood refreshment stand in my poor neighborhood. The officer stopped to chat and take a chance on purchasing a couple cups of ice cold "Kool Aid. Times have changed. I imagine that now, I as a poor kid, would be put in chains, dragged to juvenile hall by Code Enforcement Agents and Imprisoned by IRS and the State Board of Equalization (State Taxing Authority) officials for code violations and/or some type of tax evasion charge, and investigated by Homeland Security for some form of terrorist plot and non-permitted activity said "tongue in cheek" now. At that time however, our society was more supportive and encouraging to youth to be innovative and entrepreneurial. The essence of that encouragement at that time of society being that at a future date, one would start a business and contribute to society and the governments revenue. In any case, that brief conversation, discretionary patronage and trust of the highway patrol officer was encouraging and provided a foundation of my respect for professional law enforcement officers at all levels throughout life. Ironically, I became Captain of the grammar School Safety Patrol and still have the Awards Certificate signed by the local Highway Commander. I reflected back on that experience when I, as an Associate Warden addressed a large group of California Highway Patrol Officers on their training day on site at the California Institution for Men State Prison - Chino, California and received a surprising thunderous applause. As a career choice, I might have joined the Highway Patrol but had second thoughts, due to the narrow promotional command levels structure compared to the Corrections Agency.

Another positive encounter was with a city police officer on routine patrol in my childhood neighborhood who in a courteous and caring tone, counselled me on being out late on foot essentially amounting to loitering. Now officials would see little to no problem in "Hang Out" given officials now seem to condone and encourage vagrancy, loitering and camping out on public and private land.) Being an only child, I often found myself alone and on my own. On another occasion, a city police officer stopped me in a vehicle while I was on a date with a girl-friend for making an improper left turn and gave me a friendly warning.

These positively toned encounters by Caucasian law enforcement officers went a long way to demonstrate that the system could be compassionate and caring (I used the conditional phrase, "could be compassionate and caring"). I find few law-enforcement officers now who even seem to have a positive public relations personality. It seems to me now that when young officers put on the uniform their personalities become akin to that of a robot with no semblance of public relations "affect". It is then unfortunately, no wonder that the divorce rate in law-enforcement is so high; the very difficult job hasn't gotten any easier. I see the other side of the coin too however. I had good "affect" and personality but became one of those "statistics" more than my share of times.

I remembered that during my career, I occupied positions of authority and tried to reflect back on the benefit of courtesy and to solicit friendly compliance from those governed whenever possible. However, I found I could be very cold and absolutely authoritarian given my experiences, training, military service preparations and the need to do so. If my mention of the life-long positive difference to me that an act of courtesy and the difference it can make for law enforcement officers who encounter deserving Filipino youth, other minority youth and adults, then this mention has been well worth the time and has conveyed the right message.

Military Service and Related Social Experiences Broadens my Horizon

Perhaps the real change in my attitude came upon my entry into the military at the age of 17 (with parent's consent). Upon my entry into the military it became general consensus among me and my peers that "undesirables" came in all colors, ranks, forms and gradient degrees in between. The essence of discrimination became further mitigated in my mind, based on a matter of an individual looking dumb, doing dumb things, communicating inadequately and being just plain "stupid". Still, black, white or in between, I cannot remember someone in the combat zones not liking, or hating, someone because of their race. Dislike manifested itself on the basis of a personal issue and the incidental association and articulations followed to the effect that they were a stupid black, white or other. I did observe some very deep "feeling" about other races by whites originating from the south and other ethnicities harboring their own respective biases. While I was uncomfortable with such attitudes, I was somewhat relieved when in working close together on an assignment, a white fellow sailor would say something to a black sailor such as "you can't help yourself, you have a "disability" and the Black would retaliate by saying "you can't either you're a dumb white boy or "hillbilly" but each worked together to accomplish the task at hand. I was quite surprised by the candidness of such interchanges and even mutual respect for each other despite such barbs. I felt like each was saying what they really thought but weren't letting that get in the way of helping each other in spite of it. After work, they would sit and eat with each other as though nothing had ever happened. I came to respect this open matter of fact honesty more than when and where individuals really thought badly of another based on race but each would suppress letting it go any further than a basic reality. In a practical surface sense – this approach tended to mitigate deep seated hate getting in the way of working together. When I observed these situations, however, I felt uneasy and caught in the middle.

Reflections on Immigrant and Bridge Generation Survival in America

Thus far I have set out to share with the reader the true and unabridged feelings of what it was like for me and perhaps others as an offspring of a mixed-race Filipino/Caucasian marriage. I started out to share those experiences that are those of a first generation Filipino/Caucasian or Filipino, Caucasian of Northern European descent from youth to adulthood. I found I often thought white but was not accepted as such because I had brown skin.

I do not want to travel too far into sacred territory without devoting a section of this writing to American Caucasians and other individuals, groups or institutions which made first generation transition better for me in some ways and perhaps for many others as well. Regardless of the reasons for migration and assimilation difficulty of life in a new land for the Filipino immigrant in the 1920s and 30s, Filipino immigrants needed subsistence assistance to survive in a new land and they were resourceful in their survival. Life in and throughout the Philippine Islands was fundamentally adequate for most Filipinos, filled with culture, family support and hope; even contentment despite the mediocrity of life for many. These conclusions and opinions on life in the Philippines, I derived from stories from many "Manongs", friends and family and my personal visits to the Islands. Many American friends and visitors to the Philippines Island, speak of fun visits to to resorts. Unfortunately, my family 100 years ago were not familiar with resort living and plentiful staples; I did not observe such opulence on my visits to the Philippines 50 years or so ago either. Attaining menial supplies of food were the fundamental focus of Filipinos in my family who lived in rural provincial areas throughout the Philippine Islands and in the north. Those same survival skills of living off the land, farming and fishing, lent themselves to employable skills for Filipino immigrants I was familiar with upon their arrival in the western region of the United States.

Perhaps it was God's plan that the part of the United States to which most migrating Filipinos conveniently migrated to was California, a fertile and wet land similar to that of the Philippines with farming and the Alaskan fishing industry. The brutality of the hot climate in the central part of the state of California known as the San Joaquin Valley was said to be similar to the hot climates of the Philippines absent the seemingly higher humidity of most parts of the Philippines. Thus, Filipinos with a built-in survival work ethic were able to distinguish themselves as very dependable and productive crop workers. For most of them it was relatively easy to find work harvesting tree fruit and row crops. It was these same crops that made work available to the off-spring of the Filipino immigrant though these were not immigrants but the sons and daughters – even the wives of the Filipino immigrant. It was these same jobs that made work available for Filipino-Caucasian mestizo children, like me, to help support themselves through school from the sixth grade through high school. Immigrants from the Philippine Island used the formal and informal network to get jobs in the 1920's, 30's and 40's. This is still a most viable source of employment for immigrants to the United States though the service industry seems a highly viable alternative opportunity for employment and economic survival.

Intermittently as a high school student, I attempted agricultural work whenever possible. I found the work hard, repetitive and grueling. I remember one job during high-school one summer at the age of 16 working in the fields in Lodi California tipping grapes; another job in the fall planting rows and rows of onions as far as the eye could see; no restrooms or break areas. For those of us who were Filipino-Caucasian mestizos and particularly for me, I greatly appreciated the farmers that provided jobs and opportunity for field labor and pocket money. My most memorable personal experience in agricultural work in field crops came right after high school.

I remember another job picking pears in Walnut Grove and the culture shock I experienced. Living away from family in bunkhouses, up at five o'clock in the morning and partaking of breakfast of the camp cooks choosing was rigorous. The camp cooks choice was basically his selection of hot dogs, or spam, sausage, fried baloney, steamed rice and scrambled eggs with black coffee. I remember the first day of work, I wasn't too excited by the breakfast cuisine and therefore ate very little. However, by midday, I was very hungry! I didn't make that same mistake of not eating enough again! We would work in the grove picking pears all day climbing up and down twelve-foot tripod ladders we would carry from tree to tree. "First picking" was more tiresome and not very productive due to few pears large enough to select for harvest.

In the evening a couple of Caucasian "ladies" would visit the camp in the evening after dinner for those who wished to indulge in more intimate female company. The work experience was so arduous for me that I concluded that if one had any semblance of a choice, you would darn sure have selected a more traditional Chamber of Commerce touted type of American work experience if at all possible. It was here I also worked with Mexican workers out of Texas called "Braceros" (arm laborers) and learned to polish my learned Spanish language skills as we young Mestizos shared the second-floor bunkhouse with them. Though some of the Filipinos were married to Mexican women, it was obvious to us that they preferred not to live with the Mexicans.

At about 17 years of age, I really thought hard about any choices I had. One day I and a high-school buddy working with me decided that we would not go to work in the fields in the morning but draw advance piecework pay, go back to town and visit our girlfriends. As mentioned earlier, I had thought it out and decided I would look for a non-farming or harvesting job; a job out of the sun and the hot weather. Part of the decision to look for a different job stemmed from the consciousness that this outdoor labor was not what my father wanted for me and worked so hard to come to America for. I thought of the hard work and times dad had been through and the sacrifices he had made to see me through school and to high school graduation. The other part of the reality for me was that I was just too soft for the rigorous discipline and sacrifices I was making in life every day I went into the fields to work. I again do thank the American farmer, who though profit motivated, provided many a family an opportunity to earn subsistence money in order to assimilate into the United States and eventually pursue various American ways of life. Here, the good American (Caucasian) comes into play is recognized and appreciated. I don't know what comparative field work was like earlier but I imagined Larry Itliong (Filipino labor Organizer) may have had a positive influence overall in that bunkhouse living was not too bad, there was running water, outhouse restrooms and basic Filipino breakfast of scrambled eggs, fried "weiners", fried baloney and day-old steamed rice. That was much better however, than in some other field work situations where restrooms were not available. No wonder some vegetable products got tainted by e-coli!

My first effort the next day after arriving back into town, was to get cleaned up with fresh, clean clothes and visit the Unemployment Office in Stockton located one block in back of the Civic Auditorium. The dedicated Caucasian civil servant lady will not remember me nor I her. However, it was this pivotal point that my life changed as I took application in hand to "Window 7" and after a sit-down cursory interview, was sent over to the new Stockton library building for an interview. I was hired along with numerous others by a Caucasian administrator to staff the new library. For me this was a fortuitous decision. I appreciated this gentleman as being a "good" American and giving me my first hourly part-time civil service position however menial a job other people might have considered it to be. Today, there is an Unemployment Office though duties have changed so that people desiring a job, citizen or immigrant, are expected to go "on-line" to the appropriate agency to search for a job. Private labor search firms can be addressed in person or on the "net". Per my experience the most effective way to get a job is by developing a personal network and referral. As a bridge generation Mestizo-Filipino I graduated from high school really "without a clue" as to how to go about getting a job. I guess you could really say that I was lacking in the "networking" department. Looking back, network wise, most of the people I hung around with were going on to college, not to work, so there was a not too obvious to me, absence of "finding a job" conversation.

PART IV

Mental Processing of the American Experience – Reflections, Personal Achievement and Expressing Appreciation

(Transition into America for the "Bridge Generation" Mestizo)

Making sense of situations you find yourself in but do not understand can be difficult, especially when there are conflicting messages, laws and societal norms involved. This conflict can be highlighted by something one of my black friends whom I do not remember now said to me when we were post-adolescents about the American perspective on color and race: "If you're black step back, if you're brown stick around, if you're white, you're all right!". I felt bad for myself but felt even more uncomfortable for my friend who seemed to accept this as his truth. As time evolved in my life, I was more able to put discriminatory attitudes in perspective, to accept reality, mitigate the reality, and to live with it. There were people, situations and entities that were instrumental in helping me achieve a more balanced attitude to some degree.

I believe the first entity that made transition and living in the American culture better for me was the church organization in which I was brought up in and which contributed to a better self-worth identity for me. Specific to this encouragement to me were the members of the church my parents raised me in, both White, Filipino, Mexican and other who encouraged my spiritual, mental and other talent development. The church environment offered me a feeling of support, safety and friendship - with adults providing direct and indirect support, guidance and encouragement. The guidance, and support came in a sincere and humble way intended to provide a context of constructive growth and social assimilation via behavior that was acceptable and pointing out behavior which may be less than desirable. The protestant church I was raised in allowed for some individual worship participation including singing, the playing of instruments, some oratory skill and group activities participation. There was also some element of interpersonal social interaction with like-minded and similarly aged females which helped to alleviate one element of social loneliness and encourage some elements of boy – girl interest and related approved activities. Given that the church organization was statewide in California, this gave me an extended social network and the idea that there were other Filipino-Caucasian mestizos like me throughout the state. I was also encouraged by personal observations and the recognition that they were surviving if not thriving in their respective American environments.

This association with other mestizo youths, male and female, also gave me encouragement toward social interaction on a short-term basis and in some cases, friendships and personal friendships over a life-time. Because of the closeness of our parents and families, some were to become benevolent and dearer to me than a brother, or sister or other blood relations.

The next group that I want to credit and feel that most first generation offspring of immigrants in my situation should give credit to are the educators from first through the 12th grade; various teachers of all disciplines including art (skip the only *jack butt* of an art teacher I had who seemed out of his element working with minority and Caucasian students), music, math, sciences, English, speech, vocational shops, most physical education coaches and others, absent those teachers with underlying hostility toward students of Asian descent. Some teachers were truly lacking in terms of training, ability, attitude and developmental and mentoring skills where Filipino-Caucasian mestizo youth were concerned. This category of teacher is mentioned at the outset because they truly were not helpful and left on their own without the compensatory skills of their education field colleagues, would have/could have, been utterly destructive to me. In some cases, the prejudice of some teachers was easily evident. Fortunately, I did not go to "All White" schools and thus there were ample numbers of brown, black, Asian and other kids in their classes, and the school overall, for them to exact evidences of their superiority on. It was also fortunate that such teachers with evident prejudices were teaching in minority laden schools and did not have free reign to openly bestow hostilities and innate prejudicial actions toward. Had they been assigned to all white schools they might have been able to freely exact their vengeance against underrepresented minority students they found in their classes.

Most of the other teachers seemed to deal with the students objectively based on student interpersonal relationships with their teachers and academic performance. The important conclusion of my experience with teachers however, was that as a product of an illegal unison and marriage, being a Filipino-Caucasian Mestizo, I felt I was viewed as an inadequate human-being and thus I did not relate and communicate with the teachers with the confidence, comfort and ease I would have needed to in order to be seen as "adequate", social or otherwise, in their eyes. It is my feeling that teachers played, and do play, a very important behavioral role as models and nurturers for students from immigrant families most at my school seemed to rise to the occasion and were wonderful at making a difference. A few could have helped to make more of a difference but a few males teachers seemed to be in a competitive mode with male students or plainly punitive in attitude. I could be more definitive on this issue but this is not the time or place. Two instructors made a definite contribution to my life. One instructor was a male chemistry teacher John Vomocil, whose style of teaching class motivated me to excel and the other a female social studies teacher, Flora Olson, whose skill with young people and leadership brought me out of an anti-social mode and motivated me to be a young adult of pride and social interaction.

In reflecting back to my school days, one particular condemnation does stick out which occurred in the third grade. I was eating whole kernel corn from a school lunch tray with a spoon when my teacher came by me and said, seemingly in not too tactful a manner, "Al, you know you should not be eating that with your spoon". I was highly embarrassed, more by the fact that the teacher, in my mind, ridiculed me. In actually I liked this white teacher and wanted to be seen in more of a favorable light by her to some degree. In reality I felt that my whole family and way of life was being disparaged. I knew that the teacher knew I was the son of a Filipino immigrant and used to opportunity to highlight me as some kind of heathen. I remembered that moment of ridicule for a long time; it still sticks out in my mind. I learned – Words can hurt, once said, you can't take them back or undo the damage. I have tried to practice that, judicious use of words in my life, however, I have found that this is easier to say than to practice it in all cases.

I liked school. I liked school for two reason. The first reason I liked school was due to the social aspects of interaction and playing with other students of all races and of course - girls. School also provided me the foundation of a young adult mind and the fundamentals needed to be successful in interactions with other young people and to improve my social skills in addressing complex interpersonal and everyday life situations and in just living the American Dream from day to day. Being the son of a Filipino immigrant did not automatically give me the foundations for being a successful American. Being a Filipino-Caucasian mestizo American was a double whammy! My father did not have personal experience in American public schools and thus could not offer any personal survival, information for coping with the complexities of a Junior High or High School student or have an understanding of the process for preparing for, or getting into college. Consequently, I did not get pressures from home to go to college – ever – that I can remember. It was only because my friends and others were talking about going to college that I put the challenge on myself that I should go to college if I wanted to be as "good" as they were going to be for doing so. In Junior High school I remember that the school had a college career guidance day. Each student was to state what he or she was going to be. This was a laugh because I did not at all know what I wanted to be or even could be. I went to the vocational dictionary and chose the most notable title I could find. Yes, that title was Aeronautical Electronics Engineer. No one challenged me on that because at the time, few knew what that was anyway - I still laugh about the absurdity of the hoax. Such proclamation did set me up onto a college prep curriculum the rest of the way through school. However, that was the last I spoke of such a career goal.

Perspective of School in Retrospect

Looking back at school in retrospect, I feel I was proverbially thrown under the bus. The Junior and Senior High school counselors I had who were good at telling me what I could and should do (go to college) were sadly lacking in guiding me toward how would go about it; what did I need to focus on, and how to go about gaining entrance, more specifically. I could have used guidance on how to go about selecting a college and the application process. Sadly, relative to in depth counseling and guidance, I fear that I looked well kept, was relatively articulate, and pretty well dressed. Perhaps the counselors felt I had more home support and guidance than I did. As the first-generation son of an immigrant, knowledge of this process not available from the home. Telling me that I had the aptitude to be a doctor or lawyer was one thing but providing some learned insight and guidance into how I might overcome my financial difficulty to further self-actualize on those abilities was another story. They either lacked perception, training or mentoring ability to facilitate or they concluded I was just another migrant's son and I could make better on my own or would wind up working as a laborer in the fields or a cannery which is where I felt they probably thought I belonged anyway. I doubt they would have treated one of their sons, nephews or other family member so nonchalantly. Incidentally, as I recall from so many years ago, the Counselors were referred to as "Guidance Counselors". I recognize that more than a few minorities of that time did continue on directly through high-school to college with or without family money. To these students (many Filipino Caucasian Mestizos) I give kudos. Unfortunately, I am writing about my experience and for me that did not happen. If there are any student that are reading this and find themselves in a questionable or desperate position I would encourage you to go to top administration, be direct in what your problem or concern is, and ask them if them to assist you in guidance or by referring you to someone who specializes in guiding people like you through the problem at hand. As for me, I wish I had been more assertive in seeking assistance, aid and direction. I feel that one of the reasons I did not seek assistance was that I felt that because of being a Filipino-Caucasian mestizo whose parents were not approved to marry each other because of the anti-miscegenation laws, I was pushing the envelope and I was therefore did not feel worthy of being helped. As the Americans would now say "My Bad".

Speaking of Filipino role models, I did have a Filipino Spanish teacher who was kind of an anomaly as far as teachers and Filipinos went in my eyes. To that point I had not seen or known any Filipino teachers in the school system I attended. I liked him because he was Filipino which to me was a good example and someone who it would be good to relate to. However, it seemed to me that he was caught up in perhaps what a teacher might have been in the Philippine Islands and seemed too busy trying to hold his own in an American school system to relate – at all - to me a mestizo of Filipino heritage. I told my father that he called us by our last names. My father's response was simply that was the practice in the Philippines. I think I was looking for a more Americanized Filipino example and let it go at that. Ironically fifty years later I found this teacher's name in my father's citizenship Graduation Program. I believe I saw one other who was said to be a teacher of Filipino extract but again, the teacher seemed to be too busy with the personal Americanization process to sponsor a Filipino student's group. I never verified if the teacher was Filipino or of another Asian ethnicity.

House Minority Leader Kevin McCarthy greeting Viet Nam Veteran, Al Fillon, Kern County Honor Flight participant at the U.S. Capitol - Oct. 2019

College or Military Service - Hard Choices

As a Filipino – Caucasian Mestizo I felt that I should be pursuing higher education and was able to matriculate into the local two-year community college on my own. Subsequently because of personal circumstances I found I did not have enough money to comfortably attend college on my own as my parents had cut off financial assistance and the job I had was not paying enough to maintain me while going to school. Once again, the "monkey", figuratively speaking, was shoulder as I felt a little out of place. I was now out of my racial comfort racial element in junior college. Additionally, most of the students seemed more socially sophisticated than I. It seemed that my friends knew where they were headed and I had not yet found my niche. I was also spending too much time "hanging out" and socializing at the student cafeteria/study/ social area or hanging out at the End Zone student café across the street at the University of Pacific. My grades weren't good as they should have been and I knew it was just a matter of time until I would lose my deferment which would mean being ordered to active duty. Consequently, I applied to transfer from military reserves status to active duty status. I had joined the U. S. Naval Reserve in between my junior and senior year of high school. I was obligated to weekly reserve training drills for two years or sooner unless I were to drop out of school or college. If I did not meet the educational deferment requirement I would then be obligated to report for active duty. The Viet Nam conflict was heating up and Uncle Sam was only too happy to add me to the massive military build-up. I found myself immediately activated and processed for service in the Viet Nam conflict. Luckily, by the time I active I had progressed rank wise to the level of E-3 (Enlisted level 3) with approximately eighteen months of longevity for pay purposes. That was a good thing because pay at that level was quite paltry and starting off on active duty with a little extra pay, comparatively, was a small blessing.

Bakersfield Mayor Karen Goh Bidding Honor Flight Veterans, and Al
Fillion, Viet Nam Veteran, a Safe Trip to Washington D.C. Oct. 2019

Hard Times

I reported for active duty to Treasure Island for processing. I lived in
a single-story barracks, with about another 100 guys bound for active
duty. There were a lot of appointments to make, mainly for medical
and dental exams as well as personnel paperwork processing. After
administrative processing was completed, life got routine and boring
very fast. Each day companies and squads would muster on assigned
squares in front of the barracks matching an assigned number. Muster
would be called off by the Petty Officer-in-Charge and individuals
and or groups of guys would be sent somewhere on the base to work.
Incidentally, I did not receive any kitchen assignments after boot camp.
I did not like kitchen assignments in boot camp because recruits got
the dirty job and I did not like mopping and cleaning out the rooms
where large vats of food overages were stored; I always wondered how
people kept from getting sick from some kind of food poisoning due to
dirty mops being slung around by sailors who didn't give a shit; they
just wanted to get the hell out of there.

After a couple of days during processing and morning muster, I found that once they called your name and sent you off on an assignment, they didn't know what the hell happened to you until muster the next morning. To avoid work assignments, I began stepping into the number of a person called off before me. Since the number would have already been called off and the person sent off to an assignment, eventually work assignment possibilities would run out and we would be dismissed and told to police (pickup paper around the barracks and parade grounds. I would join the others pick up a few papers, work toward the outside of the area and take off for the day. I looked for recreational things to do but most recreation facilities were closed during regular work hours so I would have to get creative, go have coffee, go to the library and just kill the rest of the day. On occasion I would recruit a buddy I thought I could trust and we would find things to around the base like go watch training films or sit out at sick bay. After dinner in the evening when bored, I would put on my dress blues and head over to the Enlisted Men's club for snack, listen to band music, have a drink or two and maybe a dance or two.

Eventually, I got tired of "skating" (doing nothing) and would stay in muster formation and accept an assignment. I thought it funny that it was harder to find things to do around the base than it would be if I just went on the menial work assignments. Finally, I received my transfer document, packed my sea bag, and took the early morning bus to Oakland train bus and train terminal. By then I had become friends with a few guys and it was time to wish each other luck and shove off for parts unknown; for me it was San Diego. Being in transient in San Diego was an even bigger "cluster fuck" than Treasure Island as one of my buddies put it. There must have been thousands of Sailors and marines just milling around for days on end with nothing to do. Another of my friends joked that if LBJ (President Lyndon Baines Johnson, President at the time) knew what the hell was going on there, he would have a "shit fit". By then we had gotten our orders and were just waiting for final processing so we could head with our units to Viet Nam.

Finally, I got my "shipping out" papers and found myself headed for a ship up in up in Long Beach, an Attack Cargo Ship. I got there on a Saturday and no one knew what was going on; I surely didn't. The ship was being readied to move out to Viet Nam. All but a minimum crew was on board and the rest were all out on final days of liberty before sailing. That weekend was truly, one of the loneliest of my life. I was lucky and blessed that I had an uncle and cousins in the area so I called my uncle, A Filipino who had migrated to the United States with my father. Uncle Melicio had worked the field and performed labor in northern California. Eventually he was hired by a wealthy landowner to cook for his family. Eventually he ended up a pastor of his own church in Southern California. I found my uncle surprisingly wise and very caring. I appreciated the couple of weekends I spent at his home and his getting up early, having the coffee ready and just talking on his patio before he would take me back to the ship.

The crew returned and I was processed and assigned to Deck Force as a Boatwain's Mate striker, boat crew, underway bridge watch and truly a run of the mill "swobbie", cleanup man. Because of my aptitude scores, word got out that a new sharp guy was new onboard. Shortly thereafter I got invites from leading petty officers to join their team, mostly in technical operations. I selected Disbursing (payroll) and was allowed to obligate (strike) for it but I would have to stay on the deck force most of the time. I was the only Filipino - Caucasian American mestizo on the ship; as such, I was viewed as an anomaly - a smart guy who didn't look like anybody else but seemed to be American. The officers and some of the crew referred to me as "college boy" though I had little college at that point. Striking for a accounting clerk position was important to me and I like being a part of two different teams. Ironically, I held down several positions (billets) in supply division and remained a watch section leader in the deck force division. This was unheard of and unique given one of the billets belonged to a Caucasian guy who was pulled out of the position because "he" was being overworked, screwed over and writing his "congressman" yet I held his billet down and two others. There were some benefits, I learned a lot about survival, my capabilities compared to others peers, and along with that, I developed a strong desire to be take advantage of civilian opportunities and be successful - If I Made it Back Alive. I had a lot of duties to hold down but I liked the independence I had most of the time.

I learned a lot about life while in the military. I found that I was smarter than most of my peers; not necessarily about mechanical things or specialty items but in a sense of getting things done quickly, accurately and without a lot of supervision. I did look forward to completing my active duty obligation and getting back to school. Every day away from that goal seemed like a year. There were a couple of times I felt close to death including one day on the helm of my ship in the middle of a typhoon in the China Sea, when I said to myself, "I guess this is how I am going to die?" But, I did not die. My unit provided direct combat support in northern Viet Nam including landings at Chu Lai, Operation Double Eagle at Quang Ngai, and operational contacts in Danang. We spent much of our time running marines, supplies and military support nomenclature between the Philippines, Okinawa and Viet Nam. I visited a lot of Asian ports including several in Japan, Philippines and Hong Kong. Ironically, another very important thing I learned in the U. S. military was how to survive in the system and how to make the system work to your advantage in the American way of life. I discharged from active duty in May 1967 and remained in active drill status through June 1969 with an Honorable Discharge.

Having been pretty well indoctrinated to the military way of life, I found it to be an interesting challenge. After making Non-Commissioned Officer (NCO) circa 1968, I found service life interesting and not too difficult. With NCO chevrons and two hash marks (longevity markings) on my uniform with equivalent pay, I got little hassle from anyone, even Commissioned Officers. It was a ready-made part-time job weekly and paid by the state while on four weeks of annual active duty and paid by the state of California simultaneously. This compensation structure has now changed. As a Filipino -Caucasian American, living ethnically in two "skins", I also lived two lives: one as a civilian and one as a military-personnel. I selected a two-week active duty assignment in the summer and one usually around Christmas ending up with some pretty interesting assignments. I found if I selected my active duty during the two weeks including Christmas and New Year's, I would usually serve less than seven days on actual duty assignments. I would select administrative office duty or classroom type training in the summer two-week assignments. On my four-year active reserve re-enlistment, I occupied a Sea Bees (Construction Battalion) Billet, Naval Reserve Recruiter Billet and administrative billet as I recall Discharging again in 1973. In retrospect, my regret is that I did not actively pursue another ten years of active reserve and pursue promotion to higher rank or to Chief Warrant Officer and commensurate compensation benefits. After active duty and returning to reserve status as a Viet Nam Veteran I found that I moved freely about on military basis and assignments with little to no discrimination.

It was after my active duty discharge in 1967 that I was able to return home and to pursuit of a college degree at my hometown community college on the "GI Bill" or more accurately, on Veteran's Administration Education compensation which was sufficient to keep me going to school long enough to complete an Associate of Arts Degree. Of my college degrees, it is my feeling that my junior college classes, I most appreciated. It seemed to me that it was classes taken at that level which provided the most valuable foundations of education and personal insight into the world around me and as a springboard for upper division academic intellectualism and related work.

Another Chance to Be Successful in School
(You don't get a 2nd chance - but I did)

I served my two years of active duty and returned much more ready to return to college as a serious student. I did seem to have difficult organizing my life thoughts and being able to concentrate. After seemingly wasting two years of my life and accomplishing nothing tangible, I devoted myself toward attending college and finished an Associate of Arts Degree. I applied for Veterans Assistance, returned to the job I had before going on active duty and continued working and going to college on the "G. I Bill" (old terminology for Veterans Education Assistance Act).

I enjoyed junior college at the local community college and attended it for a long time ending up with enough units to designate a major is several areas – Social Science seemed to be broad enough to cover them all; I was proud and happy to graduate with my Associate of Arts Degree. My parents attended my graduation and were pretty proud of me also. I must say that of all the colleges I attended including upper division four-year colleges, the junior college experience in my opinion was the most meaningful to me; there I learned a lot about the basics of life. Business and economics gave me a good understanding of how the national economy works. Psychology classes gave me a lot of information of how people develop, why they behave and think the way they do. Sociology classes gave me the basics of how behavior is impacted by one's exposures, background, labelling theory, and so many other factors. The good thing about these behavioral sciences classes was that it gave me badly needed tools with which to understand my feelings and behavior and to assist myself in mitigating behavior and personal attitude(s) and healing some of the scars caused by my exposure to discrimination.

My college counselor called me in to suggest that I should seriously think about transferring to a four-year college. I transferred to the University of Pacific and enjoyed my exposure to the semi-Ivy League environment but soon transferred to a four-year State University due to financial issues. My job opportunities offered me a transfer to southern California and thus I pulled out of the community I grew up in. Luckily, I had acquired a wife and the transfer to a new community and social experience was rewarding in many ways and good for both of us. Eventually I was able to earn a Bachelor's Degree with a bit of G. I. Bill money and a bit of LEAP (Law Enforcement Assistance [grant] money).

It would be some time later before I finally earned a Master of Public Administration (MPA) degree on my own dime. I believe it was the ghost of growing up poorer and being discriminated against as a brown Filipino-Caucasian and the stigma of coming from a lesser racial composition that subliminally motivated me to earn a Master's

Degree. As a matter of fact, the ghost of that stigma seemed was again setting on my shoulder and in my face telling me as a brown skinned Filipino -Caucasian I was not good enough, still not the equivalent of the "white' American. As I look back, I can say that the stigma was always on my shoulder with that same message which drove me on to achieve another degree.

Once I achieved and was awarded the Master of Public Administration Degree, the thought of a working toward a Philosophical Doctorate Degree (PhD) came into my mind. After deliberation I felt I had several options to choose from. I considered the Doctorate, a Law degree or a Real Estate Brokers license. By this time, salary wise, I was making close to the equivalent salary of my PhD professors and thus the struggle did not seem to justify the investment at the time; I see it differently now. The Juris Doctor was of interest but I did not intend to ever practice law. I chuckled thinking that, given my personality, I would often find myself in contempt of court and maybe even disbarred anyway. I decided that the Real Estate Brokers license offer me the most liberal options and avenue to exceptional earnings. I therefore set to work to study and sit for the Real Estate Brokers license. Never having had a Real Estate Salesman's license I passed the test on the 2nd setting for it. As I sit here writing, I know that I have looked into a PhD or doctorate. However, to date I find that the schools in California that offer the PhD in the fields I would be interested in and qualified to contribute in expect one to spend several years taking regimented classes and committed schedules, not to mention a significant outlay of cash I was not likely recoup. The ridiculousness of this concept has finally tamed the inequality monkey on my back though I would still pursue it if a reasonable doctoral program or juris doctoral programs comes to my attention. I should say that I am successfully retired and would not again in this life-time hold an actual job.

Returning to my original theme, the deficiency I experienced in Mestizo student counseling also reminds me of the experience shared with me by a family member. His school counselor dismissed any desire he had to pursue upper-division college and encouraged him to instead pursue a vocational trade – not a formal college education. It just so happened that the student was strong willed enough and also had a mother who was a college graduate professional. The young man graduated from U. C. Berkeley with double Masters Degrees and went on to become professional.

Appreciating Good Americans and Mentors

As I have shared earlier, this is not intended to be a referendum bashing Caucasians or any other Americans or people for that matter. As I look back there were numerous Americans and particularly Caucasian Americans who did try to help me. I would be remiss if I did not take a moment to acknowledge and appreciate one of my Naval Reserve Commanding Officers who went the extra mile to mentor and encourage me.

I have found that if a current immigrant or the mestizo is to be successful in America, he or she will need to take very seriously any opportunity that presents itself. I did not have the mentoring I needed at the time. Thus, I know now in retrospect that I did not self-actualize and take advantage as aggressively as I should have, the opportunities afforded me. To the current immigrant, mestizo or not, this remains the best and most effective way to gain advantage, socio-economic success and fulfilling employment.

Another positive encounter came from a personnel manager for Sears Robuck's in Stockton reached out to give me an opportunity to join the organization. I was looking for an Office type job hoping to work my way up and responded to an ad in the newspaper for a clerk position in the accounting department. While I was not successful in landing that position, the manager called me personally, advised me why I did not get the position but provided a few meaningful kudos and encouraged me to give sales a chance which I did. When I reached out later to thank him for extending himself to encourage me I was advised that he had been transferred to New York. I was happy for him but sad for myself in that I felt I had lost a good person in my potential network though I did not know what a "mentor" was at that time.

A Caucasian Personnel Manager for Libby Owens Ford Class Company in Latrop, California a small rural community and site of a major glass manufacturing plant just outside of my hometown also deserves credit for encouraging me as a person whom unbeknownst to me stated that he felt I had potential for more opportunity with the company and provided a smoother assimilation into team.

As I began my career in the California Prison System, I eventually supported and mentored by a Caucasian Prison Warden/Superintendent who migrated to California from Oklahoma along with several other Oklahoman friends, in search of opportunity. This person was one who encouraged thinking outside the box and his managers were also similarly empowered. More than one Warden in the Department of Corrections provided encouragement and opportunity for me to press onward and upward. Ironically, some of the stiffest resistance to promotion and mentoring came not only from Caucasian managers but from minority men and women with "issues" that would fill a novel sized book. By the same token however, there were some that did take the time to assist me in developing my potential to succeed in the field and those I appreciated. It is worth noting that of approximately forty thousand employees with this department, Filipino-Caucasians as a whole, were not a group that was mentored and promoted; consequently, I found myself the only Filipino-Caucasian at each level I promoted to until my retirement. As far as pursuing the American Dream in state service organizations in California, this would not be a recommendation I would make even at the current time unless one is willing to be satisfied in stereotypical staffer type jobs; there may even be doctors but don't look for a command position through conventional means based on merit.

When I first joined the department fresh out of the military and broached the subject of promotions with peers, they were quick to mention that "it is all politics". I was too naïve to fully understand the concept of what they were talking about or meant – I equated politics to public official "politics" and similar concepts of public political life. It is well that a young Filipino-Caucasian person as such I was, did not fully understand the implications of this concept and such labelling. It was not too long a period of time after that, that I myself became labelled as involved in politics within the organization due to my competitive successes on state civil service promotional lists within the department in which I worked. I don't believe that being "political" was the reason for my standing out at that time. I like to think and share that I felt and do still feel that any competitive promotional successes I had was due to being clean cut, articulate, and projecting an alert responsive military bearing. I came out number 1 on the State of California Department of Corrections list the first time I competed for Correctional Sergeant. I still have to think hard on how that happened. Sadly, by the time I achieved that news, I had no one to really enthusiastically share the news with as I was going into a divorce; news of success was not something that seemed meaningful to my partner at the time. This was the unfortunate reality of growing as a off-spring of a first-generation migration; no family support, network or mentors to support or console. At some point looming in the future I would hit the glass ceiling based on "silent beefs", (innuendo based on prejudice) and career sabotage. However, social, marital and relationship adjustment for the Filipino-Mestizo is a topic that could fill a book; a number of novels, fiction and non-fiction works.

Though eligible I did not readily seek highest level command positions until the end of my career. I did make relatively steady progress promoting upward over the years however. My pursuit of the golden goose in that context is a story all its own which will be told in a separate future works. At the end of my career when close to or at retirement age, when I was finally offered higher level positions, I put my ego behind me and refused them; but my refusals were not out of anger, disappointment or spite. I had many options ahead including an offer for a Wardens job in private prison; I looked forward to new challenges. Ironically however, I figured I had been the same person for a number of years while in senior management with an abundance of experience and proven capabilities in prison management and correctional operations, however I felt I was not selected for serious consideration at the time. I was dismayed that the system was not more objective in selecting its higher-level managers. I could articulate a whole host of specific examples, where Caucasians or other competitors were not held to the same high standard of performance, experience, professional standards and conduct as I had maintained. At some point it may periodically appear that I leading the reader to a feeling that this book is only about negative experience with the "white man", that is not the case. There were many Caucasians in my life that were the best of friends, as well as nurturing and helpful. But without them my life would be amiss and absent a lot of happiness and success. These are the wonderful! This manuscript does point out a unique unpleasant side of people that the Filipino-Caucasian was better off to leave behind or never to have encountered.

Reader Caveat

(If you are reading this book, I assume that you are not only interested in experiential situations of difficulty, challenge and overcoming. However, I have found that there are things one can do to better prepare themselves for the conflicts of racism they may encounter. There are other things the reader may be able to do which may help them avoid the conflict altogether. The "Caveats" I added in, in order to share with the reader, some knowledge, information, or methods of addressing situations which I may have utilized or items of personal awareness I learned. By taking advantage of this "life coaching" the reader or immigrant reading this book does may not have to re-invent the wheel" of life in order to have a more orderly life than I had and consequently a quicker route to success.)

In the previous paragraph, I shared a little of my experience with you regarding the importance of maintaining a good rapport with ones' supervisor and the value of being mentored.

I will share with you my finding that regardless how high or important a person in your chain of command is, or how high his or her position may be in your organization, do not be surprised by just how fragile that persons ego may be; as fragile as an eggshell. I found that you will do yourself a favor in any organization, if you recognize that natural and common human frailness; that you are prepared for it and, are also careful with your contrarian personal opinions, suggestions and conclusions. Think about the ramifications of a point you want to make, before you act or speak. Further, just like an eggshell, once you cause doubt as to your loyalty or a fissure or crack in the eggshell, it cannot be undone. Think of it in this way. As a minority, is the point you want to make worth jeopardizing your personal success and promotability, your interpersonal relationships in the organization, or the financial security and well-being of your family over? I found this a good analytical example to apply to my personal life and to live by as well.

Filipino-Caucasian Demographics in my Work Environment

I started my career 33 year Corrections career at Stockton, California working at Deuel Vocational Institution – Tracy in 1968. At that time in a staff of approximately 400, there were only two others of Filipino heritage, one Filipino and one mestizo – Filipino/Caucasian; I became the third one. (1)

A sample of visible ethnic compositions of line command staff in several of the numerous other California Prisons at the time I worked at over them over a 33 year period of my adult career were as follows:

- 1972 Calif. State Prison Jamestown Ca. Staff 500 1 Filipino 2 Mexican, 2 Blacks,
- 1974 Calif. State Prison Norco, Ca. Staff 650 1 Filipino, 1 Mestizo Filipino/Caucasian*
- 1975 Calif. State Prison Chino, Ca. Staff 450 1 Filipino, 1 Fil/ Mex. 1 Fil/Caucasian *
- 1990 Calif. Women's Prison Madera Ca. Staff 1 200 2 Filipino Other Ethnics Significant*
- 1992 Calif. State Prison Chino, Ca. Staff 1,200 4 Filipino Other Ethnics – Significant*

- 1996 Calif State Prison Wasco Ca. Staff 1,205 4 Filipino Other Ethnics - Significant*
- Parole Div. So. Calif Region. Staff 405 2 Filipino, 1 Fil/Cauc. Other Ethnics - Significant*

The Parole and Community Services referred to by field staff and the public as "Paroles" was comprised of Four Regions in California with Region IV composed of the Counties of San Diego, Imperial, Riverside, San Bernardino, Orange and the eastern part of Los Angeles County. Again, the use of the term "Significant" for Black and Mexican Employees I used due to the fact that employment quotas were established by the States Affirmative Action program to ensure recruitment and filling of significant numbers of position by those ethnicities. There was also a quota for female employees. At the time, no quota existed for Filipinos. Filipinos were lumped in with Asians and Pacific Islanders. As an Affirmative Action /EEO (Equal Employment Opportunity Officer I would see this group total one percent (1%) and that would not raise an eyebrow of any administrator.

(1) Staffing is a close approximations based on personal knowledge as a Correctional Management Trainee, Assistant Training Officer and personal observation.

*Other staff are shown as "Significant" show as such in that the staffing label of Mexican and Black were benefitted by enacted laws related to Affirmative Action. As such, minimum quotas were established by California Law and adhered to even to the detriment of other ethnicities including Asian and Filipino for which no allowances or quotas were established. I have spoken earlier to a specific experience I had wherein the Warden had no Filipino Correctional Lieutenants but told me he would hire a Black and a Mexican but already had too many Filipinos. He had absolutely no Filipinos or Filipino Mestizos filling any of the 25 Correctional Lieutenant positions. This occurred in approximately 1976. When I interviewed for an Assistant Deputy Director - Institutions Division Position in 1998 there were no Filipinos at that level and there are still none as of this writing to my knowledge. I would be would be willing to bet one lunch that there will not be any from the ranks during my life time unless this writing stirs action in that direction. I would hope it does It still seems to be the same old story, "No Dogs or Filipinos Need Apply Here" regardless Executive Action.

If you refer to page 61 you will find that I took a six year self-imposed career development break from the California Department of Correction's Institution Division which comprised itself of approximately thirty prisons and after fourteen years in the prison system took a lateral transfer from working in prisons into the Community "Paroles" Division. The

PART V

Socio-Political Experiences and Reflections of a Filipino-Caucasian American

Sociological Truths as I see Them in Assimilating into America or Some Straight Talk on "Kicking Butt" American and not so American Style

There are many views regarding how to best and most effectively assimilate into the American culture for an immigrant and that immigrant's sons or daughters. From this Mestizo's point of view the bottom line is to excel in every area you find yourself involved in. It's going to be about winning, coming out on top in everything you do. In the classroom, in the gym, on the job, on the number of widgets you produce, on the ball field or on the high school debate team. It is all about coming out number one. In academic performance, in physical competition, in all matters of achievement, out-performing someone else, another American or anybody – that is what it all boils down to. That sounds good, noble and "American".

It is no secret that I worked in a large bureaucracy with the State of California, specifically, the California Department of Corrections for approximately 32.9 years. There are many experiences and encounters and confrontations that could be highlighted, dissected and analyzed relative. However, this is not the time and place as to do so would detract from the main theme of this thesis.

I joined the Corrections agency shortly after returning from military service. I had worked at the manufacturing plant where I had worked briefly before and after military service. I was happy to find that by taking military leave of absence before going on active duty I accrued seniority and had a pretty decent position on returning. Leaving the large manufacturing plant was a gut-wrenching decision. At the plant I had enough seniority to be able to work in the evenings and go to college in the day. For many reasons however, it turned out to be a most fortuitous decision. By going to school during the day, I felt like a regular college student and that was really a great feeling. By having a good paying job while going to school I also I did not feel as strapped for money as I had felt while attending college before I went on active duty.

Alfonso K. Fillon MPA

Socio-Political Impediments in Hiring
of the Filipino-Caucasian Mestizo

As I approached senior high school my father encouraged me to look into becoming a policeman or fireman. In retrospect, I have concluded that my father did not fully understand how difficult it would be for a brown skinned Filipino-Caucasian American to be accepted in a fire department. Even now, I have never seen a brown skinned person in a command position in fire departments of any agency. What I do see and the public seems pacified by, are persons of color and maybe even female, acting as a public agency spokesperson. The unsuspecting public assumes that because they see a person of color on television or at public events or featured at community service organizations as speakers, or a person with a Spanish or Filipino surname speaking on behalf of a public agency quoted in headlines, that this is representative of the agency's <u>Command</u> structure composition. In my experience over the years, nothing could be further from the truth! I always assume that what I see in action is "B S" window dressing until proven otherwise. My father's hope was that I would be able to secure a civil service position which had sick leave, vacation, decent working conditions and a retirement system compared to working in the fields with no such benefits; line level "gopher" worker bee jobs, yes, that was possible. I was impressed with the idea of having a job with an agency under civil service guidelines and thus accepted an appointment into the corrections department as a Correctional Officer. I had applied at the California Youth Authority for a position as a Group Counselor. For me to attain Civil Service employment, its security and many related benefits that was the reason my father tried very hard to keep me out of trouble. However, in this case, I did not fit the desired profile for the kind of person the hiring panel felt would be a good fit. Because I was recently out of the military (a Viet Nam Veteran), I was viewed as likely to be too rigid in enforcing rules. I concluded that their agency representative did not feel I, as a Filipino-Caucasian mestizo, could relate to their juvenile client base; was to gentle to "mix it up" and they were not willing to waste their time giving a different looking person an opportunity. I concluded that because in their minds, I was not a Mexican, and in their mind, I did not speak Spanish (which I did however) and I obviously was not black they were not interested in me. I was later able to talk to one of the panel members in a social situation and able to find my intuition to be validated; the curse of being "different" – I would see this again and again in other contexts and settings over the years. Several of my friends and college colleagues worked there as did my college compatriot who had just discharged from the Marines. We were able to compare notes and laugh over a beer. Perhaps the one benefit I felt cheated on was not being able to study college courses at night while the wards were "down" (locked up for the night) as my college friends were able to do in those positions. Along these lines, approximately five years later I was to become involved in recruitment for the sister agency and the Career Opportunity Development section of the California State Personnel Board and we were making every possible effort to recruit "the kind of people" this department seemed not interested in earlier.

The Department of Corrections (the Adult Prison System) was a different world compared to the world of the Youth Authority which ironically, no longer exist. For one thing, the job of a Correctional Officer was not as cushy as those in the positions occupied by my friends over at the Youth Authority. Consequently, recruitment was a little more difficult and the job considered dangerous. Several of my fellow officers and friends did end up being killed on duty over the years. At the time of initial employment, a number of my friends and colleagues even suggested I was crazy for going "over there". I was offered and did accept a position and was given the opportunity to be placed on the evening "Watch" (shift) if I would/could complete one week of day shift for orientation purposes. Thus, I did find employment close to home in Stockton California, at Deuel Vocational Institution Tracy, California. On the third day of employment, I remembered going home in the evening, lying on my back on the bed and asking myself why and what had I done to myself in accepting the job. It appeared I was somewhat out of my element. However, I did meet another Filipino-Caucasian mestizo Correctional Officer (Guard) who was quite knowledgeable and experienced and that did help to calm my anxieties about whether or not I might fit. Ironically this associate transferred to the Youth Authority as a supervisor and while he encouraged me to try again I did not. Having just gotten out of the service I liked being in uniform and related well to the para-military rank structure and existence of a clear chain of command. Interested in attaining promotional rank as quickly as possible, I competed for, and was placed on, a number of promotional lists. My first promotion was as a Correctional Program Supervisor position at the Sierra Conservation Center, Jamestown, California. The announcement appeared in the Stockton Record; very few people took notice. That was the first of a number of positions I was to promote into throughout the state of California. In retrospect, I have some sadness in not growing with the community and being a part of its growth. Over 40 years, I adapted to a number of communities and work environments. However, I was so distracted by attempting to put down roots as I moved about the state of California, having worked in about 14 of thirty four prison and numerous parole office sites through the state, that I feel I lost some of my foundation as a son of a Filipino immigrant to some degree over that period of time. The mechanics of ones geographical movement is relatively easy to collect and document. What is difficult, is capturing the humanness of it all. The, physical moves, the relocation and assimilation into the communities, the differences in people, area customs, demographic variations and culture; these are the elements that tend to diffuse your foundations and psychological roots; emotional attachment sites upon which to build a full life on. These are the things that based on my psyche and emotion, I missed out on. Coming back to my home town and the Filipino community I left is both a relaxant and a stimulant to me. In the twilight of years, I look forward to making the most of new opportunities and options. A 1969 graduate of San Joaquin Delta College and a member of the student planning committee, I have not yet been on the award-winning campus; I look forward and hope to find that it and the other new complexes around town are Senior Citizen friendly.

The town I grew up in is gone! The dry goods stores, jewelry stores, men and women's clothing stores and counter restaurants, the "5 and 10", - all are gone. The sites are either boarded up in a state of disrepair or torn down and replaced by massive structures that are either not drawing business or are not conducive to business induced foot traffic while parking options seem to leave a lot to be desired.

Bureaucracies and the Socio-Political Gauntlet in Promotions

As I have stated in other parts of this writing my career was not always smooth. I have also shared the limited number of Filipinos and or - Filipino Caucasians working in the various institution workforces at which I worked over time; the percentage of Filipino staff compared to the full workforce was miniscule if existent at all. Many Caucasian staff members were comfortable in "bullying" other employees who would allow it and especially "Chinks" as I was often referred to as. There were no EEO (Equal Employment Officers) and anyone with any authority of review would label you weak and not fit for service in this business. As a matter of fact, they hoped that you would complain about "something" so they could hang a label or "silent beef" on you. In some way, shape or form, you would read about it on your performance report in the context "lack of ability to adapt to work expectations" or "get along with other employees". I was able to breakout of the pack when a newly envisioned called Correctional Management Trainee Series was implemented which required demonstrated academic and management potential aptitude which I was able to successfully qualify for. Despite additional hurdles of discrimination fostered by the program, I was able to complete levels I through III. After these promotions, I became eligible for promotion to Correctional Management Trainee IV, the final rung on the ladder and equivalent to Correctional Lieutenant. At that level I found myself vying for a vacant position at a different institution (prison) in southern California.

I was encouraged by Corrections headquarters staff to approach the Warden of an institution in the area with two Correctional Lieutenant vacant positions. Thus, I scheduled an appointment with the Warden to request consideration for one of the positions. The Warden was very straightforward and not reluctant to inform me that there were in fact two positions open but the first position would be filled by a Black person and the second would be filled by a "Chicano" – that if the first position was filled by a "Chicano" the second position would be filled by a Black person. I was somewhat astounded by this behavior and bold articulation of intent to discriminate. To this I asked the Warden, "How about a person of Filipino heritage – how would I factor into the consideration equation?". To which he responded, "We have too many already!". In reality there were no Filipino's in the uniformed staff and with this attitude there would be none! I had made up my mind however, that I would not settle for being summarily dismissed from consideration in what I considered a subjective game I was caught in and a reverse play using reverse affirmation action; Affirmative Action being a very valid and viable hiring concept at the time.

Per my observation, the Affirmative Action programs and quotas were of little benefit to Asians and those of Filipino descent: absolute worthless and no help where I was concerned. Given that the Warden was being so candid and forthright with his tirade, I asked him, hoping for an honest and direct answer, How do you feel about me? – hypothetically, "if I were to be in the position, would you have a problem with me working for you?". To this the Warden indicated "No, he would not'. He further went on to say that he did not see how that would ever be possible as Wardens run their own prisons. I then courteously thanked him for his time and any consideration and excused myself. I smiled softly inside knowing that he had laid down a gauntly and/ or mine field for me to pass through but I was not through and knew I would be taking this option to a higher level. Subsequently, while on relaxing vacation in Las Vegas, I was contacted by headquarters and informed that an arrangement had been worked out; I was given a reporting date to his prison.

Two Sides of the Ethical Coin of Embedded Organizational Discrimination in Action

Years later the shoe of watching the system discriminate would be on my foot. A peer Black Administrator and myself were on a hiring panel. The peer panel member felt the best candidate for the job would be an older Black man. The gentleman would be working for one of us and either of us would have been happy to have him working with us. Although we expected some backlash, given prior hiring preference patterns, we submitted him for hire. After submitting the gentleman's name with a recommendation to hire to the top Division Black administrator, a decision came back that he, in fact, would not be hired. When my co-panel member associate and I inquired as to why not, the response was that the top administrator who again, was a Black man, thought he was "too old". We shook our heads in disbelief and walked out the door. Luckily for the "too old" Black gentleman, another vacancy occurred which forced a reluctant hire. There were numerous other instances of discrimination and fostering of a hostile working environment created by this administrator. Eventually his blatant incompetence was "outed" on a nationally syndicated and aired television show. Subsequently, he was demoted to a lesser level for one reason or another. I was to find out later via a retired Deputy Director and other employees and managers that he continued to "poison the well" against me. I am grateful to other administrators, White, Black and Brown who saw him and his ranting and raving for what they were and yet were willing and strong enough to stand tall, and also were ethical enough to make decisions based on integrity, objectivity and performance. These types of people I consider a blessing to people of color like me, and to their families, communities and organizations for whom they worked.

Author in Full Attire and Regalia as Worthy President,
Fraternal Order of Eagles Aeriee #93 Bakersfield, Calif
with Viet Nam military medals (circa 2004)

The Filipino-Caucasian Mestizo and Political Aspirations

I did have occasion to run for public office as a member of the city school district in Riverside, Ca. While I was not successful, I did learn a lot about community political processes. In retrospect, I feel I was naïve to not think that being a Filipino-Caucasian mestizo would not be a factor. As a matter of fact, I paid little attention to it in my strategy; a big mistake. Consequently, I do not feel that I was politically sophisticated enough to effectively compete at that time and did not yet have my Master's Degree. In that election process, I came in about fourth of six candidates for three vacant positions. However, I enjoyed going through the process, meeting the people and the dynamics related to running for a community office. I do feel that I did learn what I did not do and could have/should have done to be a more viable candidate and quite likely elected. I did apply for a community position on the City of Riverside Board of Administrative Appeals and was selected to serve. That was a great experience and again I learned a lot about community politics, political processes and how boards and commissions functions. At that time and maybe because of my ego and self-confidence, I did not have feelings of personal, financial or racial inadequacy or inequality. In retrospect, I feel that in that period of life my ego was bigger than the person. I can probably say that at that time, for a number of reasons, I felt on top of the world. It was a good feeling to have. In some ways however, the aforementioned situation runs a little contrary to the behavioral grain. I was raised to stay very focused and that being number one was good. The dichotomy of this was that I was also raised to be reserved, respectful and to not make waves. Being reserved may have been based on a cultural norm, but being reserved in aspiring to leadership can get in the way of competition and winning in America. I found a personal foundation of morality to be unequivocally important; it was the most important element of my character. Though on occasions I greatly suffered because of it, I would not have wanted to be without out it. I found it to be my saving grace, when I had nothing and no one left standing with me that I could rely on.

Caveats for Young and Adult Readers of all backgrounds

In my childhood rearing by my parents, I was expected to be serious and focused. I found my father liked to enjoy situations and have fun; he could have been more fun. It is too bad that my father had to, at least in his own mind, concentrate so heavily on making a living and trying to live up to his perceptions of what an American should be. My father had a saying, "Don't be too happy cause then you'll be sad." I do not know or truly understand his motivation behind that saying though I have heard similar expressions in Eastern philosophy. I took it to mean that moderation was the best personal mood path to follow. I do not have that cross to bear; I am an American. I am the epitome of an American absent skin color. Still, as a Filipino-Caucasian American, I feel that it is important for us to be to be taken serious and business like by our American observers; to stay focused on skills development, time management and achieving written goals and objectives. and had main office and Absolute effective communication skills, written and verbal, and direct eye to eye contact are tremendously important.

Many of these skills, you may learn in college but that is only the tip of the iceberg. Superior verbal communication is a must if you want to be competitive and stand out. Those of superior intellect and those of lesser intellect will recognize your social and intellectual achievement by virtue of your ability to communicate: do it well. I found in my life as a Filipino-Caucasian American that while you may not come out number one in all of your competitive endeavors, if you don't take no for an answer, you are most likely to eventually succeed. If you do accept "no" to pursuing and fulfilling your dreams, or, are not willing to have faith in yourself - you are guaranteed to not self-actualize your dreams.

As the son of a Filipino immigrant in the period of time I was raised, 1940s and 50's, I was taught to be respectful and not create waves, (not even small ripples). Why? Because if you stood out, it would cause the "American" to come after you in one way or another, no matter what your standing in the community may be. If your skin is not white, the established white or "real" American, will come at you to take you down a notch or more, when you least expect it from and angle where you will least expect it. We only have to look as close as our nightly news to see that even the "real American" will fall victim to the bureaucracy when they least expect it.! Regardless of your political affiliation - is Lieutenant General Flynn one of those victims? I suggest that if he, as a life-time military and political bureaucrat didn't see it coming, what is the likelihood that a first-generation Filipino Caucasian mestizo with a modicum of power or on the lower end of the bureaucratic continuum would be able to have an effective "firewall" from the system or in any organization. Yes, time for another "On Guard".

Community Fraternal Organizations in the Life of a Filipino-Caucasian Mestizo

I gained some valuable experiences in and about White Americans, their various cultures, personality quirks, personal biases, prejudices and many other idiosyncrasies in joining semi-public benevolent lodges such as the Benevolent and Protective Order of Elks, (per Wikipedia, this organization was originally an all-white organization until 1976), and the Loyal Order of Moose, and, the Fraternal Order of Eagles. In each of these organizations, I had friends of white and of color that belonged to these various organizations. The Fraternal Order of Eagles was the first organization I join and eventually matriculated through the hierarchy of officer positions or "chairs" (levels of position) to President and the stature of Worthy Past President of the local Lodge. This was followed by membership in two consecutive lodges of the Benevolent and Protective Order of Elks occupying a minor officer positions followed by membership in two consecutive lodge memberships of the Loyal Order of Moose. The consecutive memberships was due to geographical transfers and a desire to be a member of the home lodge in the area I lived in. My experience in each of the Lodges was average, I had no one ever address me negatively though I always expected that it was a possibility. However, I believe I carried myself in a warm, friendly dignified manner and allowed people to get to know me at their own pace and as they chose, or not. Those who were overly garrulous or given to imbibing excessive "spirits", I courteously avoided. I visited various lodges throughout the states as a member-guest: I did not remain at, or revisit any that I felt the least bit uncomfortable at. Each of the organizations and even individual lodges, throughout the nation, had a different benevolent/social aspect to them. Just as in any roadhouse or "bar and grill", I found there are friendly and unfriendly people, for whatever reason. I tended to guide my behavior and attitude In these environments as "live and let live". However, because of the various charters extolling - equality, justice, helping others, brotherhood, sisterhood etcetera, there exists for the most part, a real effort to welcome newcomers regardless of differences, especially if you are prone to be involved in, or sponsor, a charity; a big plus to almost universal acceptance. As a Filipino-Caucasian mestizo, a seemingly real minority in these organizations, I would encourage looking into membership of one or more organizations of your choice in order to broaden you exposure to others, and to allow Caucasians to get to know you as an individual first, and then a positive representative of your respective ethnic background. In this local community setting I learned a lot about "things", social, technical, or even hobbies and sports or just community business, that I was not particularly familiar with. I considered joining one of the veteran's organizations but was a little "turned off" by what seemed like occasional and unpredictable over-militarization, self-aggrandizement and reliving of war stories, occasional loose language, and sporadic focus on negative experiences with the "VA" (Veterans Administration". As a veteran, I feel an obligation to support one and believe I have found one in my home town I would live to support with my membership.

Author and Shannon Grove, Calif. State Assembly (circa 2014); now Minority Leader, Calif State Senate

Motivational Coaches Can Make a World of Difference and Change your Life -It Did Mine

In the world and particularly in the United States, there are numerous motivational speakers and writers. I was fortunate to share interest in one motivational guru by a learned associate, himself a writer. While many motivational gurus talk about the power of written goals and objectives, this particular motivational leader had a particular way of driving home the importance of written goals and objectives and the method by which they can and do make a difference between following through and achieving your dreams and simply searching for your dreams. The particular motivational guru and life or success coach I am speaking of is Anthony Robbins (Robbins Research Intl, San Diego Calif.). Many years ago I was responsible for law enforcement operational sites for the agency I worked for throughout southern California from San Diego to Imperial County, Orange County, East Los Angeles to Riverside County to San Bernardino and Victorville to the East; 17 sites and 22 offices in all and a vast geography. On the days I had regional administrative officer of the day duty and other days by choice, my commute was mainly between Santa Ana in Orange County and Riverside in Riverside County; a distance of approximately 40 miles. I had a large span of control and a lot of responsibility. On certain days I would decide to schedule my San Diego office management trips to San Diego and on certain days of the month I would schedule my office management visits to Palm Springs or simply remain in Orange County or Los Angeles for dinner, etc. The world seemed like my oyster so to speak. When I left the Institution (Prisons) Division, I was counselled to not stay out in field services too long, my mentors would "forget about me". One day I was sitting on a shady bench at the marina adjacent to Seaport Village in San Diego after a seafood lunch, nibbling on buttered popcorn with a icy soda on watching yachts sail by and joyful vacationers from all over the world walking happily arm and arm along the water, some with children floating colored balloons straining for the sky. I couldn't believe that "a little brown bastard" as the white

American called me when I was a child in Stockton California was actually getting paid to partake of this ambience; many people would have considered it the equivalent of an all-expenses paid vacation. On that particular day however, I was "pondering".

I had been called the previous day by a professional associate who came up through the ranks with me and informed me the information was strictly confidential; that "vetting" was in the final stages of being announced as the new Prison Warden for a prison under construction; that he was putting his team together; that as a part of that, he would like me to take the job under him as Chief of Operations for the build out and construction of a new prison; that several people (competitors) were being thrown in the mix but I was viewed based on previous institution experience as amply qualified and perhaps preferred, if I could make it through the politics of the selection process. Previously, I had been offered several such jobs as this in the Institutions Division prior to taking the one I was now in as District Administrator - Field Services Division but each time, I had excused myself for one reason or another from participating in the selection process. Supervising a team of managers, my responsibility would be liaison with the project management company, ordering supplies and equipment similar to that you would find in a city, from paperclips to guns and bullets, all operational post orders and job descriptions, operational vehicles, staff and inmate supplies, you name it. I would also be responsible for hiring into 1,200 positions from Correctional Officers counselors managers, ensuring adequate training, and establishment of a staffing schedule called a master roster with which to staff the institution for around the clock operation 365 days a year, feeding and inmate work assignments and service and supervision of 2,800 inmates at excess capacity and an annual operational budget of $138 million a year. So, what was I pondering? I knew that before I had gone into field- services I would have been up to the task of starting a new prison on 640 acres of what was agricultural land from the ground up and through day to day operation and relished the idea. But now, I had to ask myself, did I really have it in me?

Previously I had prided myself as a prison-operations expert. But in reality, I had not personally met the challenge and taken advantage of the opportunity to activate a prison from the ground up. Yes, I had a cushy job, but as I analyzed where I was now compared where, mentally and emotionally, I had been in the past when I was on a path to success and feeling challenged and unstoppable, I was now in a Division where people were content to remain in cushy jobs and just be liked by the bosses in order to keep them; to stay where they were inside the proverbial little white picket fence of safety and perceived security playing itself and making no waves, I had even began to doubt myself and my ability. Perhaps the self-analyzation process first started when I had been reachable on a promotional list but was interviewed by a Deputy Director on the fast track. This person had no previous line experience in institution operations and comparatively, minimal education yet was promoted into a high-level management position and then quickly promoted into the field-services operation. It was this minimally experienced person that I found chairing my promotional opportunity interview and selected another person with little line experience also. It didn't take much to see that I was allowing bureaucratic gamesmanship or personal vendettas to be involved in decisions that were being made over my life and consequently stifling my personal ability and creativity. I asked myself, where was the little boy that teachers touted over saying he (I) was very smart and should be a doctor or lawyer?

If you are wondering if I am telling the truth about the deficit managerial state of affairs in that division I worked in at the time, I can only refer you to your computer's search engine site and the information explaining inadequate staff and administrators performance and the reasons for a $20 million dollar settlement on behalf of Jaycee Druggard, a notorious case in which a young female child was kidnapped and living in the back yard of a California parolee, likely an interstate compact agreement case. The numerous articles on the details of neglect that lead to the continuing of eighteen years of abuse of the victim are clearly delineated for anyone to digest. Standards of supervision were routinely violated during overseeing of the case. Such was the state of affairs in that division and lack of attention to managerial detail at the time, in my insider experiences and opinion. I remember one colleague, telling, me "don't try to make any changes, if you do, the change will be you" and he chuckled. It was good advice which I took into serious consideration. I would have difficulty getting the man's or woman's "knee off my neck". I found that in bureaucratic agencies, Executive level administrators tend to identify with a fad, in this case, using their clout in a public agency to be popular with subsets of personnel that they have left themselves vulnerable to, or compromised with, and then use their position to attempt to right their wrong or compensate for their human and organizational weak spots. Often times, such social experiments, organizational malfeasance and absence of true ethical standards on their part goes unchallenged - even unnoticed by their superiors, who themselves are playing the same game. But, every once in a while, their shenanigans, unethical, errant management style, and lack of personal and organizational integrity, as I have alluded to earlier, catches up with them. When it does, great financial penalties are exacted, paid out of the pockets of the tax payers; money that could have been used to help real and honest people. When I followed this case through the courts, the state assembly and state senate that approved the $20 million dollar payment, I saw no names associated with the negligent behavior, no forensic breakdown as to responsible parties and mis-performance relative to standards of practices - only highlighting of reasons and precedents to excuse non-performance. While I am on this subject, I recently listened to a book on CD by former governor Jesse Ventura, American Conspiracies, (Jesse Ventura and Dick Russell 2010 Tantor Media, Inc.) As one reviewer wrote, *"You may not believe everything in American Conspiracies, but it is guaranteed to make you think harder about the things you do believe".* If only 30 percent of the things are true, it is no wonder that Americans felt empowered to demean Filipinos and Filipino-Caucasian mestizo Americans at will.

Back to my thesis statements however, it was on one of the 40 mile hour-and-a-half commutes home from Orange County to Riverside while I was relistening to motivational tapes from Anthony Robbin's, Personal Power, series about unlocking the Personal Power (to achieve) within and mulling over what I had let myself become and subordinated myself to that I decided "No More!" At that awakening moment, I made the final decision to not be trapped on an experimental management merry go round or maze any longer; I would break away from the "man" with his "knee on my neck". (I believe that Anthony Robbins does have a CD, Awaken the Giant Within - worth it's weight in gold to me). When the call came for a scheduled interview, I accepted it without hesitation. I interviewed with vigor and enthusiasm as though my life depended on it: it did! As he chuckled, I ran the Tony Robbins motivational tape information through my head and decided that if the job offer came through, I would accept it. Twenty plus years have passed, yet I still cannot forget the quagmire of hopelessness I observed at the time and subsequently motivated me to get back on the personal high road.

I was successful in the interview process and was on my way to a new life. I always believed in continuing to invest in yourself and self-improvement; the minor expense of investing in self-improvement courses or related reading, I always found to be well worth the money spent. (By the way, in my opinion, no one makes a bigger believer in yourself than Tony Robbins and his Motivational Programs as he takes you from his driving a little Volkswagen Bug to owning a personal jet).

Many of these skills utilized in my interview, you may learn in college but that is only the tip of the iceberg. Superior verbal communication is a must if you want to be competitive and stand out as a Filipino-Caucasian mestizo; most of the Filipino -Caucasian mestizos I have observed have mastered this skill very well and thus have become very successful. Those Americans of superior intellect and those of lesser intellect will recognize your social and intellectual achievement by virtue of your ability to communicate: do it well. While you may not come out number one in all of your competitive endeavors, if you don't take no for an answer, you will eventually succeed. As the son of a Filipino immigrant in the period of time I was raised, I was taught to be respectful and not create waves, (not even small ripples). Why? Because if you stood out, it would cause the "American" to come after you no matter what your standing in the community may be. If your skin is not white, the established white American will come at you when you least expect it and from an angle where you will least expect it.

At the present time we are seeing a good example of this in the United States where the President has been too "forward" and too brash with his personal financial accomplishments. Ironically, of all the minorities, Filipinos and Filipino-Caucasians in the United States, none, per the current United States President, are seemingly knowledgeable and otherwise capable of performing at the Cabinet level in the United States government. So, it would appear that the pendulum has swung in the other direction - away from equal representation in government. I feel that this highlights my point that I would not recommend government service if you are desirous of rising to the top position of a government agency. If you are, be prepared to put all of your cards on the table and be prepared to risk it all. A good example is Lt. General Michael Flynn, National Security Advisor nominee, who, although white, was targeted, subdued and financially broken after a stellar government career. When analyzing my position on excelling do not get sidetracked with politics or emotion. The example is made, even now, Do Not Stand Out – (publicly). You will be "marked" and "They" will come for you – when you least expect it.

Though most Filipinos in the 1930 and 1940 were field or domestic workers, many would come to town in suits, white shirts and ties and polished shoes on Saturday nights to dance with "white taxi dancers" in the dance halls. That engendered further hostility of the white Americans. Work camps were raided with the intent of hanging Filipinos; a miscegenation law was passed in an attempt prevent Filipinos from getting a marriage license to marry white women in the state of California. Filipinos were accused of affiliating with white churches so they could "get" white women. In another case exhibiting the anti-miscegenation law, my cousin writes of a requirement for her mother (of Mexican-American descent) and her father (Filipino) to visit another state to obtain a marriage license.

On Winning

In my opinion and experience, the American way of winning is to appear gentlemanly almost as though you really did not want to win the respective contest (unless you are a politician). I went to a grandson's baseball game in San Francisco and the attitude of the team, some of the parents and the coaches I observed (and was told) as well, was "not to win by too much". I was chastised by a family member for encouraging my grandson to run and take additional bases as the other team not being used to the pressure, was going bonkers, overthrowing the ball at each base. That laisse faire attitude about winning drove me Nuts!!! I haven't been invited back for any competitive games involving my grandchildren since. Professional sports seems to be an exception to the rule wherein the end justifies the means.

Now, back to the point. In general, it is my opinion that if you are an immigrant and do not want to be overtly discriminated against and attacked when you are at the top of your game, on selected occasions, it may be better to appear, low-keyed, almost apologetic. Be "Humble" to bring less attention to yourself. You should remember that it is more likely than not that because you are "of color" (Filipino-Caucasian mestizo) your opinion and behavior will always (more likely than not) be "circumspect". Your opinions on subjects and matters are likely to be viewed by "Caucasian-Americans" as lacking full understanding, not having depth, lacking in experience on the subject matter, and/or in some other way, not credible or valid. The essence of this on the Filipino-Caucasian mestizo is that if you are learned and self-confident enough to accept the likelihood of this supposition, then you will take extra time whenever possible to study, research, analyze all aspects and likely have the better conclusions/decisions. Still in all - you will find that you are still under the cloud of an unfavorable label. I found this to be true in many situations throughout my life a a Filipino Caucasian mestizo.

I was invited to attend a hiring night exercise at a private University. I found that the participants were mostly all Type A personalities willing to rudely talk over others for personal recognition and to stand out looking for acceptance and making the final cut. Caucasian participants felt empowered to "talk over" Asian participants and me included with condoning of the facilitator. After the exercise was over, I did not wait for the results as during the process I had decided that this was not my kind of place and that my personal culture ethics and morality would not be a good fit in this organization. To me, it was a forum for the "Ugly American" prototype" which I did not fit into comfortably. I had "arrived" and felt that to be in this organization would demand that I chronically re-assert and engage in re-validating myself among others with lesser standing and experience. I felt that I had put it all together and that perhaps I had gotten a step closer to getting the monkey of inequality off my back.

Caveat

I found that in attempting to overcome inequality and discrimination you will probably want to do a lot of self-study, read a lot of "How To" and Self-Improvement type books", I did. These included sociological and psychological adaptation advice books; books like "How to Negotiate Anything" for example. When you get good enough at it you will eventually be able to come out on top of most situations of conflict. When you do achieve comparative success, you will know that you are on the right track. That was a great feeling for me. What else can you do? Resist the temptation to show discomfort, anger desire retribution. No, don't turn the other cheek. But what you can do is look for allies who see it your way, your point of view and who have proven credibility. Solicit tactfully their support. Get better at handling conflict, disagreements, etc. As a Filipino-Caucasian Mestizo, these are some of the techniques I had to get good at. Still, I found that I am what I am a Filipino-Caucasian mestizo. As such, you and your point of view will generally not be respected or appreciated. Get used to it, learn to cope with it. Accept that such conflict is inevitable. Know that you are valid and have integrity. It helps if and when, your detractor comes to your truth (golden nugget) on their own; it will take more than once for you to be validated in their mind.

Another Level of Over-coming Sociological Inequality – Personal Economics

It is my feeling that a brown skinned -immigrant and Mestizo cannot personally overcome severity of racial discrimination at least in their mind without paying some attention to financial stability. Financial stability will likely give you the means to have the basics and "enjoy" some of the American Dream elements while you develop a plan to assimilate and navigate through the social system.

This is not a treatise on achieving financial success but as a matter of mitigating the psychological harm of discrimination I reflect back and feel that the immigrant and first-generation mestizo must pay some attention to improving their financial status. Most of my peers have done amazingly well. In retrospect, however, this is one area I should have been more aggressively focused on earlier in life and once focused never let up. To be successful as a Filipino-Caucasian Mestizo person you will need to master financial concepts and learn how to amass a good cash bank account. One should be fanatical about legally accomplishing this even if it means a part-time second job to get there beginning early in life and career. I believe that learning how to maximize your earning potential and being able to live within your means can make a real difference in the comfort level of just living life. I had to go out of my way to learn this and then to practice it. Otherwise it would have never happened. I learned late in life that you can trade your way to a six-figure income. The sooner you learn and embrace this concept, the sooner a better socioeconomic life will be yours. I, personally, wish I had learned and applied this concept much earlier in life. However, as a first-generation mestizo and son of a Filipino immigrant, untutored in sophisticated real American economic survival and/or success, I did not learn this. I and most people innately apply the standard of overwhelming financial success to conventional means such as a pay raise, of which most are miniscule; longevity pay, merit salary increases or a windfall of cash (in heritance or a large jackpot at the local casino). I will perhaps include more on this in one of my future books but for now, broaching this idea with the reader is most likely sufficient.

Living Within Our Means!!

As the son of a dedicated honorable Filipino immigrant who toiled at mostly minimum paying jobs, the use of credit was an important survival too! As a child, I remember going to my uncle's grocery store, a neighborhood market on the outskirts of town and selecting food items. In some ways, this seemed exciting. It was an old and friendly store with ample space and close parking. Best of all, uncle was very friendly and dad could carry on conversations and discuss news from the Philippines while shopping for groceries. On these occasions, mom and dad seemed a little more liberal on the selection of food items. I was always happy to get a bag of chips or an ice-cream bar. Uncle would often toss in vegetables and fruit that hadn't sold and we would enjoy a good dinner.

A Hard but Benevolent Lesson on Credit Cards for a First-Generation Mestizo Filipino

Later in life after leaving home and returning from military service, I desired to purchase a sporty type used automobile in good shape but with a few years on it. Like many people even today, I did not have cash for the amount and thus had to go to my friendly branch of the Bank of America for a personal loan. Having only recently returned from active duty, I had limited savings. In the process, I felt that the "friendly" banker turned out to not be so friendly after all. As a matter of fact, I found him quite rude and insulting making unnecessary pronouncements as to my lack of credit worthiness based on a cursory review of a standard personal loan application. Needless to say, I did not get the loan. Nor did I close out my checking account, cut up my credit card or close out my Safe Deposit Box with a few documents and about $600 dollars of savings bonds in it. You" remember that at some point I mentioned the school savings program managed by Bank America any my weekly contributions to savings. It was not until later in life and the fact that I no longer needed credit. It came to me that if I could go just one month without using a credit card, I would no longer need credit! I also recognized that if I could eliminate the build-up of a credit card balance, I could actually eliminate the credit card use fee and interest. I also realized that some banks had programs that would give (credit) you "travel miles"; that you could earn these travel miles and not accumulate the credit fee and interest nor have to carry over a balance and still use the card during the month for convenience sake. I went to paying cash for goods and services and paying off the monthly balance in the given grace period. Finally, I learned to cut my ties with the "unfriendly" banker's bank where I felt taken for granted and began using the services of a credit unions. If you as a first-generation Filipino-American, do not know and "feel" the difference between a bank and a credit union, I urge you to give your self a crash course in the topic. This is a personal rule I adopted on the use of commercial services: If I cannot/do not, feel respected and appreciated - you will not see this Brown-skinned person in or around your establishment.

Credit is more likely than not, a mask of further enslavement. It will come down to not how much money you make, but – how much of what you make you actually save. I have seen this American tragedy played out many times in my life by friends and employees and have helped facilitate a number of people in restructuring their debt and financial obligations to avoid bankruptcy and foreclosure. Preservation of financial capital is a number one concept in my mind toward success and self- actualization in your community. Capital appreciation is the second of three poles in my financial success element: amassing a semi-liquid balance, retaining principle and thirdly, striving for the highest real return on your money in any investment. Growing up as a Mestizo in my community the "elegance" of really secure financial status and standing was an element missing from my environment and as such it was a hurdle I continually struggled to overcome. It was the basis of my insecurity, the in your face mirror of social and financial inadequacy that nurtured the underlying despair of almost all of my susceptibility to discrimination. I look at my salary or money in hand in this manner. Whatever I can put away today and have five, ten, twenty or fifty years from now, at the best interest rate I can hunt down and maintain, that money will be mine forever. This worked best when I could identify it as a matter of percentage (5%, 10%, 15%, 20% or more) of my gross pay as mine for the rest of my life. It just keeps on giving like the battery advertised that powers the bunny.

Remembrances About Personal Appearance and Socio-Economic Aura as a Youth

Appearances do make a difference for most everyone but young movie stars it seems. There is a saying initiated by a motivational speaker/innovator many years ago, I am not sure who. It goes this way. "You only get one chance to make a First Impression". I was very impressed with pictures of well-dressed Filipinos in America in the 1930s, 40s and 50s including Filipinos dressed for my father and mother's wedding. I remember that my father outside of his work clothes usually wore a white shirt, tie, slacks and often a hat and thus was generally respected. I followed suite, dressing neatly for school and took pride in keeping my clothes up, clean and pressed often wearing a buttoned-down collared shirt, tie, slacks, the most expensive "looking" cardigan sweater I could afford and polished shoes. I found it just as inexpensive to dress neatly as it was to dress in "play clothes". Luckily, most of my peers wore similar nice clothes took the same meticulous care of their clothes and regardless did not ostracize me. Once in a while, I might get subtle feedback close to home, to the effect as, "who did I think I was" dressing nicely. but I was so seemingly cash poor that I regarded any such comments as a real compliment. Looking spiffy was important to me, I tried my best. I really did enjoy sweatshirts on occasional dress-down days, however. Dad thought corduroy pants were the in thing but I did not like them or wear them much. Ironically, one of my female classmates recently told me that they remembered me in what else - corduroy pants! How ironic!

At twelve years of age I was able to get a job as a paper carrier for the local newspaper. I was really proud of the money I made to augment my meager allowance. I was particularly pleased with the freedom and independence that I was afforded due to this job. The monetary reward, numerous valuable prizes, fast food coupon and excursions I earned really augmented my quality of life. As a young poor boy there were only a few things I desired. The desired items were a bicycle, a Daisy B B gun and a television. Televisions were not common to most households and not a priority to my parents. With the money from my paper route I was able to work a payment deal out with my mother and thus purchase a television that used "Rabbit Ears" for channel reception. There were only four channels on the television at that time and most were off by mid-night. Being an only child, the television brought countless hours of entertainment into my life. Being a first generation Filipino-Caucasian mestizo, viewing the television brought many experiences and exposures to the American way of life to me including social behavioral experiences, modeling of expected social conduct, as well as political insights via nightly news.

One day when I came home from school there was an old balloon-tired bicycle sitting on its kickstand on the walkway on the way into the house. Upon entering the house, I was afraid to ask to whom the bicycle might belong lest my hope that it was for me be obliterated. As I sat down to the table for dinner, I still kept hoping that it was for me - but I was still afraid to ask about its ownership until my parents asked me how I liked it. Of course, the old used red bike made me happy and opened up a whole new life adventure for me as I used it to go everywhere and to run grocery errands for my mother and father. It also opened up a many new experiences and adventures for me as I and my best neighborhood friend Ben rode all over the streets of Stockton on our bicycles. I am familiar with some children or young people close to me who would not be happy with a bicycle unless it is brand new – top quality and brand –"How things have changed"!!! I did not think twice about it being used or painted over. As a matter of contrast, in recent years when I asked about a bicycle for my grandson, I was told that my grandson only wanted a certain high-priced brand or nothing. Years passed and I was able to use the bicycle to become a substitute paper carrier and eventually have my own paying route: I was a happy Mestizo!!!

I remember that at some point my father had gotten a second part-time job that just seemed to fall into his lap" and which really fit conveniently into the schedule around his regular job. With my father's additional income my mother (God Bless her) was able to raise my allowance which I really appreciated.

Caveat

Briefs on Personal Economics Learned from Youth and Applied

However, it is important not to squander money on expendable common goods and cheap looking clothing. You must resist the temptation to purchase depreciating assets like cars, boats and the like. If you must have an auto for example, it is best to look for dependability versus luxury that can cost extra, hard earned, and limited cash. While you are amassing cash, even a dependable previously owned vehicle is a good way to avoid depleting hard earned cash and thus have it, to put to better use purchasing appreciating assets like silver and gold, rentals or equities. I have saved countless dollars observing this practice. Remember, in America, Cash is King! Have a lot of it!!! As a preadolescent a mature Black man, one of my newspaper customers I talked with a lot told me, "Junior, if you have money, it won't make any difference what color your are – if a woman sees you have money no matter what color she is, You are the man for her". I didn't understand what he meant at the time but eventually I got the drift. A Caucasian Real Estate mentor later in life shared with me, "You know the saying, Money talks, Bullshit walks." It was difficulty to accept the reality, but eventually in life, the power of having money sank in.

Cash is King for another Reason - It can be Critical to your Least Expected Fight for Equality and Organizational Justice

In another section of this writing I share information on inequality in organizations and speak to the fact (in my mind) that if you, a Brown skinned person gain unexpected entrance into an organization but have not had time to get in good with the "good old boys or allow them to compromise your personal and organizational ethics "they" will come after you. I share this from personal experience. Perhaps, you cannot imagine the extreme levels of hate that exist and thrive in a bureaucratic organization. I will share a brief example here and likely include further examples and specifics in a book I plan to do on organization behavior.t a point in my career I sought out and took advantage of an opportunity to gain experience in a large division of the department I worked for. During that period of time I found there were a number of employees who shared overt biases about me coming taking a lateral management position into the division at a high level. As time went on, I found that there were supervisors and employees from outside of my span of supervision who began to coalesce to scrutinize operations in my area of operations. Surprising to me was the tone of the allegation against me but that also is a story for another organizational survival book. I did find that I was being spied on by a piece officer on his own time who had ironically lost his badge and wallet in my neighborhood. For this I did write a complaint. Ironically, this supervisor

Relative to this subject of money, I learned and I share - learn from the beginning to live within your means and actually below your means. This may be difficult at first but it will have a lifetime of benefit and reward. I have been writing and will publish a guide to achieving financial success for the average person. Numerous methods of overcoming financial mediocrity are included in the book. One of my Caucasian teachers in business taught us to remember to make a payment to yourself first out of each paycheck or commission, to never draw it out. Insist on always preserving and never losing principle. At a minimum understand the cash earning, "Rule of 72", and always protect your investment capital. These ideas seem to be a universal caveat among "money people".

Caveat: Drive a New Car to Impress?

Finally, I found that a bridge generation immigrant can get a handle up financially in American society by trying to ensure they buy appreciating assets versus depreciating assets. Autos depreciate! If you buy an $65,000 auto, how much actual cash value will you be able to salvage from it in five years? "New is only new while the auto is on the showroom floor. Once you sign the papers and start the engine, it is a "used" auto. If you are able to purchase an almost top of the line, dependable, year old auto with warranty, low mileage and all the bells and whistles for $35,000 that additional $30,000 savings can be invested and earn a desirable return year after year for the rest of your life. You may need an experienced financial planner's counsel to maximize the potential return on your investment. Be careful, there are a lot of phonies and professional fund managers that are complete losers but still getting paid millions for bad advice! I have practiced futility whenever possible for a life time. A Caucasian friend and business attorney mentor set the tone for my reconciliation of this issue while I was still young when he said, "Al, don't be too impressed when you see people driving new flashy cars. Most people are driving their entire net worth down the highway.". Taken to heart, these sacrifices can pay off.

As a child I participated in a passbook account with one of the local banks whose representative would pick up a student's contribution weekly. I never amassed much but it was a good experience and helped to develop good financial habits and personal expectations throughout my life. I felt good if I had any change at all to enclose in my pass book account; I made it a point to do so. Ironically it was one area that I did not feel discrimination in. I did not feel the effects of financial inequality until later in life.

However, following my personal savings and investment strategies, I began to amass a good balance over 30 plus years; enough to make me feel pretty comfortable among friends, colleagues and "strangers" of any economic strata. It is not that it made me feel better that anyone else. The self-accomplished security helped me to put the stigma of poverty behind me, appreciate my friends and others and have a benevolent heart. This was one milestone of psychic accomplishment for a brown-skinned mestizo son of a Filipino migrant referred to as a "little brown bastard" by one or more white Americans on the streets of Stockton as a little boy growing up.

Tribute to American Businessman Cleverness and Cunning

One thing as a Filipino-Caucasian Mestizo which intrigued me was the way that Americans tended to mentor their children and friends. I have observed that the American seems to have an innate sense of cunning when it comes to maintaining the status quo of culture, ownership or succession in an organization that, per my observation, the Filipino culture I was exposed to seems not to have developed or practiced I have reasoned that we as immigrants generally are too new to have sizeable ownerships of businesses, stock equities, and organizations to pass on to off-spring successors. I have also thought that the lack of mentorship is because most first or subsequent generations of immigrants are workers or professionals with what amounts to jobs such as technicians, doctors or teachers. Even so, I have observed that Caucasian Americans in business or organizations are seemingly always thinking of who they will pass their gain, position of ownership or organizational status on to. Such bequeathing is obvious in family companies. However, I have seen such planning by mentoring or even treachery in public service structures and organizations as well.

I have observed minorities and mestizos seek a top position in an organization thinking they have done all the right things, had superior credentials, experience and performance reports only to watch someone from the undeclared "inner circle" receive the elevation to top positions. I have observed such chessboard successor planning by Caucasian Americans begin years in advance even if just to prevent an "outsider" or brown person, from gaining the power position. In a comparative sense, I have not observed or read of such organized planning within most visible Filipino organizations. As a matter of fact, I have seen what I felt was just the opposite, a failure to support and mentor within and a tendency for Filipino peers in public service and government to be not supported; left on their own to "sink or swim". As a Filipino-Caucasian mestizo, mentorship and support networking with designated objectives is not an academic course I received in school, but I and others might have fared better in organizational life; future generations of immigrants may benefit likewise.

Along these lines there were educated professional Filipinos who preceded my father's migratory wave of the 1920s and 30s but the impression verbalized from many of the migrating Filipinos of that era was that they were looked down on by the preceding or educated migrants as "second-class Filipinos" – a seeming unspoken caste system. Ironically, this attitude seemed acceptable because Filipinos with "positions" were respected, even honored by the new immigrants I had been told and observed. What I did not see or feel as a Filipino -Caucasian Mestizo was the benevolent reciprocation and mentoring of the newer immigrant – my father's wave or the "bridge" generation such as I was.

Upper Left Top and Bottom: Author in Fatigues at Coyote Canyon,, Camp Pendleton, Marine Base, Ca. Upper Right: Author Junior In High School, Lower Right: Author in Dress Blues For Qtr. Deck duty - Sasebo, Japan

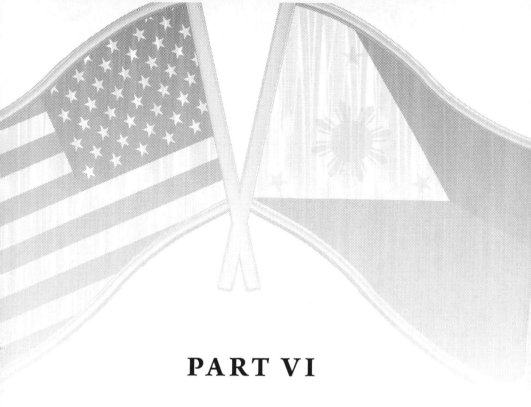

PART VI

Prejudice from Filipinos toward Filipino-Mestizos

"You're not a real Filipino" (on Illocanos –
"They eat ears, don't they!")

Growing up a Filipino-Caucasian American placed a lot of stress on me and I believe from talking to others like me, that growing up in the same ethnic composition context placed a lot of inner conflict and mental disarray on them also. The idea of thinking you are something, an American and then having that all undermined by Caucasian Americans discriminating against you; Americans referring to you as a brown bastard, a monkey and in other demeaning terms. That was a very difficult thing for me to resolve, and to put in perspective. In reality, such deprecating references and experiences did cause me shame, embarrassment, sorrow, identity ambivalence, anxiety and anger. I found myself pondering what will even the score. What will make me right? I concluded that nothing can erase it, but there are things I can do or experience that will make me feel better about myself, and potentially alleviate most of the sting of discrimination. Essentially the conclusions I came up with were subtle, indirect but in essence, quite meaningful. That meant being at the top where ever I might be and rising above others economically. This was to be a lifelong struggle more easily identifiable than achievable.

The first thing I had to do was to be sure that my head and my efforts were in order and achieved. I remained open to pursuing the truth however it might come. One such opportunity came while I was young while in the U. S. military. My father had always bragged on the goodness of the Filipinos of the Illocano dialect. On the other hand, I received and perceived some indications to the contrary from other sources. Personally, I felt an affinity for all of Filipino ethnicity.

During my time on active duty aboard a U. S. Navy Attack Cargo Ship assigned to amphibious operations in the Pacific and Viet Nam during the Viet Nam conflict, I lived in the Supply Division Quarters and also worked for a Filipino E-6 Petty Officer. Because of this living arrangement I interacted with a number of Filipinos and particular numerous Filipino Stewards from various locations throughout the Philippine Islands who provided a variety of services such as janitorial, living quarters cleaning, cooking, serving, table and kitchen cleaning and the like to the Commissioned Officers. In my own mind I felt like these positions were legitimized paid slave positions for the

Commissioned Officers - elite. I was told that the Navy would not allow Native Filipinos to enter the Navy except in these entry positions. It appears that many years later this exclusion/limitation policy was changed. In any case, I was able to spend a lot of time with these Filipinos and to visit their families in various areas of the Philippines.

I noticed that few of the Stewards were of the Ilocano speaking dialect which would generally be from the Northern part of the Philippines. I also noticed that I was regarded as very different being half white and half "Filipino – a mestizo. I was able to openly communicate with most of them and asked what their real thoughts were about the "Ilocanos". I was surprised to find that they good naturedly shared that Ilocanos had a reputation for being stingy; that Ilocanos would eat (human, I believe) "ears". I never found or understood the basis for this stereotype and may never. I cannot remember other stereotypes shared with me. However, I was really surprised by this. My father had always given me the impression that the Ilocanos as a group were a great Filipino culture. Being half Ilocano, I found that assertation convenient and desirable to accept. So much for that! It appeared, and I concluded that Filipino peers "forgave" me for being of another Filipino faction and we all went about our business trying to help each other when and if we could. In all cases they were very friendly, helpful and kind to me despite such unexpected bias differences. For that I was and am very appreciative, I try to pass it forward whenever I have an opportunity.

I remember being in bars in the Navy liberty town of Olongapo, Philippines with its dirt streets and colorful highly decorated "Jeepneys" running military personnel and others up and down the streets when female hostesses of Filipino ancestry would come up to fraternize with me as they would any military man. However, when they finally realized I was of partial Filipino ancestry, they would subtly move on to the next sailor leaving me feeling not worthwhile in their eyes. They were more than willing to befriend and talk with white sailors and marines at the bar; but not with me. By their reaction to me I felt as though I was an undercover agent and I had been "outed" (true identity discovered). In reality, I would have actually liked to talk with one or more of these ladies in order to get a better understanding of their outlook, culture, etcetera. However, their desire to be good ambassadors appeared to be more along the line of a hustle of one kind or another. I'll leave insinuations and conclusions regarding the situation to the reader. I like to think there was a modicum of subliminal respect for my father's culture and his son involved in the snub. I could have used the company just as equally as the other servicemen. However, I was highly insulted by what I considered blatant insult, rude and discourteous behavior. I felt that my negative impression was affirmed, they were only out to swindle the servicemen out of monetary compensation. I understand that "business is business". Yet to this day, I am left with a lifelong negative impression in my psyche about that experience.

I reflect back to remember a couple of times in the service while in Viet Nam waters preparing for debarkation on combat operations, I was asked by some of the usually less educated and crude Caucasian peers if I was getting ready to go over and visit my "slant eyed gook cousins". These insinuations reminded me of earlier feelings of prejudice; they were hurtful and quite frankly pissed me off. These comments from my own military comrades did not help me to resolve the inner issues of being discriminated against and being a "real" American.

Back in Japan I felt discriminated against as an American in Navy uniform noticing that the Japanese people would stare at me. I also felt that their smiles were smiles of a demeaning nature and ridicule; not of friendliness. I do not know this to be a fact – it was my perception leading to an opinion and conclusion. I hope I was wrong. I do remember that while in Sasebo Japan there was a protest going on regarding the visiting of a nuclear-powered submarine base and thus there we were not allowed to go off of the base in uniform. Consequently, I stayed on the base and had limited and filtered Japanese cultural experiences there with Japanese employed on the base. In fairness, maybe the smiles staring on such encounters had something to do with the social environment at the time. Later, I was to conclude that this behavior could likely be because I was an anomaly; an Asian looking individual in an American Navy uniform. In the Philippines however, I found my cousin and friend to be a little reluctant to be associated in public with me when I was in uniform. I was also surprised when my cousins had to intervene in Manila because the Filipino cab driver was dishonest about the fare to a destination when I was in uniform. The behavior of the cab driver was very disappointing to me. I have had to haggle issues on cab fares on occasion almost all over the world. But because of the pride my father instilled in me about the Philippines and its people, this situation hurt me very deeply.

Discrimination of a More Surprising, Personal and Devastating Nature (Intra-Cultural Bias and Prejudice)

The experience of bias and prejudice is always devastating and degrading to the recipient to some degree depending on their respective perceptions. You can somewhat rationalize it and thus mentally mitigate the impact of it when it is directed toward you from the outside of your racial composition or skin color; from a person of a dissimilar culture or race. However, when that racial discrimination come at you from someone of a culture and race you consider yourself to be a part of, that discrimination is extremely disconcerting. In such a context, you are extremely mentally dismayed, disoriented and caught by a real surprise.

I would have been better prepared to mentally process this if I had experienced this as a child in the school system at one level or another. However, my first experience with this was as a young adult. I was at a social occasion and was asked by a female (Filipina) about my nationality – was I Filipino? I replied in the affirmative that I was as I had always done given that psychologically I had selected this as the ethnicity I chose to associate myself and be associated with. I was asked further if I was "pure" Filipino to which I responded that my mother was Irish. The person went on to exclaim in what I perceived to be a demeaning fashion, "Oh, you are not a "real" Filipino! This reaction I experienced on a number of similar occasions. During a conversation with my cousin, a Filipino – Mexican mestizo I shared this experience. My cousin in southern California and a pastor of a church related to me that he had a similar experience at a bank with a bank teller while depositing money at the bank. He related that he was asked by the

Filipina bank teller if he was of Filipino heritage to which he replied that he was - but was mestizo. The teller asked him if he spoke his dialect (Ilocano). When he replied that he was not fluent in the language the teller in an admonishing tone exclaimed "Oh, you are not a real Filipino!". I had a similar experience with the exception that the person asked me in a bit of broken English if I "speak the language". I replied I did not (without explanation as to why) to which she exclaimed, "ah you are not a real Filipino!" I simply shook my head, chuckled to myself and went on my way. I will go further into analyzing this or another book at a later date. I would like to think that the intent was not one of intended insult but of simply ignorance of how that phrase is interpreted as one of insult by the perceiver. I did learn to speak Spanish rather fluently. For many reasons, it has appeared that I fit into that culture quite well, am very fond of it and have had several Spanish speaking wives and/or partners. At some point I would like to get the opportunity to discuss the language, cultural implication with a Filipino philosophical doctor in language and culture for more clarity and understanding. I do not really understand the correlation between someone not "speaking the language" and thus not being a "real" Filipino. I wondered then, if an Eskimo speaks the "language", then that person would be considered a real Filipino, but I would not be. Though I was fraught with more than a little disappointment to put it in simple, nice terms, or upset by the ridicule of me by this person, I wondered if, with her broken English, she considered herself American? If so, I guess I would be able to tell her that because her English was little better than my understanding of the Illocano dialect, that she was not a real American. While in my own mind, I felt that would not be a nice or necessary thing to say to her, and I would be feel hurt for her feeling if I were to say such a thing to her, she had no trouble at all, and no hesitation telling me I was not a real Filipino. I have also noticed that over the years, having associated with so many peer level male Filipinos, that while they might ask if I spoke a dialect, the male Filipinos were very courteous and seemingly reluctant to make issue of it. It has always seemed that the male Filipinos were courteous and respectful, and content to let the fact that I did not speak the language fluently, speak for itself. From my American point of view however, it has seemed to me as though from the female Filipino point of view, it was important to point out that I was no better than an American idiot because I did not speak the language. I know that in life, we, or at least I, learn something -if not many new things every day. I know there is a reason for the point of view and I am open and eager to learn what that reason or misperception I have is based on.

However, as a matter of reasoning, I should elaborate that I do know that from my father's viewpoint, he did not see a benefit for his children to learn the language of the Filipino. In his mind he did not want me to be regarded as a Filipino with all of the American ridicule that went with it, but an American in as many ways as possible. I can only empathize with my father and his many experiences over the years trying to learn in a haphazard way, the correct pronunciation of words, meanings of phrases and colloquialisms of the English language. I can only imagine the giggles, laughs and wonderments expressed by his Caucasian classmate in classes while attending four years of Bible College in San Francisco at a man viewed as truly out of his element in their minds. This was almost the same attitude I experienced as a youth when I was in school and thought that a couple of the girls in my class or school were cute and thus tried to be friendly. Their response to my mixed Caucasian and Filipino racial mixture seemed to be one of shame on my behalf for me being of a mixed race! At the time, I did not understand it. Now I think – Really!!!??? Now I have grown; proud of my heritage and comfortable with my uniqueness.

The seeming obliviousness and lack of sensitivity by many Filipinos and others in modern day America to the experiences of early Filipino immigrants to the United States involving the various forms and elements of ridicule and danger faced by them in their daily lives trying to become "Americans" often amazes me. This brings to mind a not so atypical incident suffered by many Filipinos but this one involving my father During the time my father attended Bible College in San Francisco (circa 1938) he was walking down Market street to a church meeting in broad daylight with another Filipino classmate when he was hit on the head from behind and knocked out by sailor in uniform calling him a "Damn Jap".

To my father's credit, he was supportive and encouraging of me when I joined the Navy at seventeen years of age. The attack on my father was but another indignity suffered at the hands of an American who, by virtue of his exclamation, did not know one Asian from another. I am thus truly bewildered by the impact these experiences of my father and the wave of migrant Filipinos of the pre-bridge generation (the 1920, 30's 40's) had on me and other members of the "bridge" generation. I am very often still devastated by the lack of knowledge and empathy many modern Filipinos have, and exhibit for, the many tremendous difficulties and degradations that vintage Filipinos experienced in their quest to become Americans. I am privileged to have learned of their struggles and indignities suffered first-hand through listening to the many Filipinos associates of my father as over time. Their willingness to share their beneficial experiences and successes with each other helped to encourage one another to continue the plight and overcome difficulties they experienced while raising families and attempting to participate in the American dream.

PART VII

Self-Actualization – Accomplishment and Reward of being Filipino-Caucasian Mestizo

Military Service Gives me an Enlightened Experience

Going on active duty in the military did give me a more enlightened experience of self-worth and an introduction as to what really makes the difference. Once in the fleet I found that Caucasian Department heads somehow through their network were looking for "strikers" (men to learn their naval job function specialty). I found that I got a few requests to talk with various department heads to see if I might be interested in being a part of their department or division. I made the choice to join the Division and Department I thought right for me. It was in the service I found that I was a little smarter overall than the average peer, had more versatility, initiative. I felt the service taught me how to "break out of the pack" and that rank would move me up from the commoners at the lower ranks and give me a more associative sense of more "elitism".

Here was a dichotomy. Throughout my life, on one hand I found myself being discriminated by Caucasian Americans in what I considered my own country America, because of my mother being "American" and on the other hand I found myself being and feeling discriminated against by members of my father's "race" Filipino in the Philippines in this context and in other situations which I will highlight later.

Definitive Factors of Change – Education, Mental Attitude and Situational Modification

Perhaps my real personal breakout had to do with availability of dates with Caucasian women after discharge from military service upon returning to college and the work force. In these situations, I found myself appreciated and related to courteously by Caucasian women, perhaps as a novelty, though I desired to interpret the interactions as ones of sincerity. It was sometimes difficult to understand "real" sincere, meanings of interest sometimes by women of minority cultures at times also. Despite a search for a mate of mixed race like myself (Filipino and European ancestry) I was unable to find a match or even someone of mixed race to consider. Thus, I became open to available

Caucasian women as well as to women of various other cultures and ethnicities. As time went on and I dated more Caucasian women during my younger years and throughout life, I was impressed with the ease at which women of the Caucasian culture moved about so freely in society without having to have any reservation or consideration as to any discriminatory and were so readily accepted. I observed that they were most always at ease in communication with other Caucasians, male and female (professional or not) and confident of their position in social situations and society in general - seemingly universally. They did not have to overcome indifferences of other Caucasians as a matter of their being better by virtue of status, culture or origin; they simply labeled the indifferent person as ignorant and /or "stupid" to say the least. I was impressed with their ability and willingness to call issues as they saw them to be, honestly and not far off the mark.

Ironically my next two wives were blonde and blue–eyed. Based on my personal life experience I did find that such mixed-race marriages in the modern era came with a number of subtle, as well as not so subtle, differences to adjust to on the part of both parties. Some of these differences had to do with adjustments on behalf of my mates; other differences had to do with recognitions of needs for adjustments of personal and cultural practices and attitudes about life and accommodations of each other. Some of these differences I chalked up to each person having rather normal differences of opinions on things, actions and behavior. What was different was the occasional differences on perspectives about race and culture – even related political perspectives. It goes without saying that after visiting a Filipino buffet type restaurant with them that neither they or I was not passionate about eating fish with heads on them, blood meat (diniguan), pig belly (bituka) and bagoong (odorous fishy seasoning paste) and other delicacies in their presence. These items were not so palatable to them and other Caucasian Americans I dated. On one occasion in Manila, Philippine Islands, accepted the challenge at a Doctors home while visiting my cousins when I ate several baloot (unhatched baby chicken in the shell with only the beak and feet formed) with San Miguel beer. To the squeamish American reader, once past the thought of eating something different, it actually was rather tasty. When I was in the service and in the port town of Olongapo P. I. I observed numerous brave sailors and marines enroute to or from the Viet Nam conflict expose themselves to sampling this tasty item along with their beverages in bars along the dusty streets.

In terms of Caucasian partners attitudes about relationships, I was very surprised that at least two of them had been in long term marriages and had known for a long time (years) that they would be leaving their spouses immediately after their last child graduated from high school. I did not know if this was a particular nuance of the Caucasian culture or just a coincidence. However, once finding this out, I was henceforth more mentally careful about making further commitments, personal and financial, in these and other relationships. My mother and father's relationship and marriage was seemingly "for better or worse" as they would occasionally joke. I was taken by surprise in that modern relationships, seemingly within the Caucasian culture were "for better only".

My Filipino female cousin asked me why I did not date Filipina women, to which I responded from the "gut" that they seemed to prefer Caucasian men for boyfriends and husbands given my experience in life and particularly after observation at a church congregation, and with career peers, friends, and events with associates who were in mixed marriages. Perhaps there is some of the same dynamics for the Filipina in these liaisons with Caucasian mates as I had described from my perspective in the preceding paragraph. I did date a number of women who were either pure Filipino or were Filipino mestizas however. In a comfort sense relative to my ethnic composition I did find that I was most surprisingly comfortable with women of the Filipino/ Caucasian mixture as they seemed to understand and easily related to my experiences and emotions of being discriminated against by both Caucasians and Filipinos. It was surprising to hear them express the same sentiments about not accepted as "real" Filipinos by many Filipinos and not real American's by members of the Caucasian race (male and female). However, each has expressed a softer tone of discrimination from those of the white population chuckling that they were readily pursued and desired by men of the white and other ethnic groups.

As a Filipino-Caucasian mestizo and exposed to the many experiences of discrimination I was exposed to because of ethnic mixture I came to feel that I should really be looking for a partner of "my own kind". This idea was easier thought (said) than done as there were so few female mestizas and the ones that were available seemed to be oblivious to the ethnic mixture matchup idea. In reality with a different criteria of raging hormones active in me at that youthful age the American "pin-up" image seemed to trump the ethnic likeness idea. Consequently, I gave up and went with the flow common for most youth of my age – femininity and sexuality. Thus, I can really relate to the position most Filipino immigrants found themselves in given there were few Filipino women of average socio-economics who during that period migrated to the United States that could be considered for wives. Thus, many Filipinos, like my father, married women they found here in the United States of the Caucasian, Mexican or other ethnicity forming the basis for mestizo children of which I am proud to be one of.

Discrimination of a More Personal and Devastating Nature (Intra-Cultural Bias and Prejudice)

The experience of bias and prejudice is always devastating and degrading to the recipient to some degree depending on their respective perceptions. You can somewhat rationalize it and thus mentally mitigate the impact of it when it is directed toward you from the outside of your racial composition or skin color; from a person of a dissimilar culture or race. However, when that racial discrimination come at you from someone of a culture and race you consider yourself to be a part of, that discrimination is extremely disconcerting. In such a context, you are extremely mentally dismayed, disoriented and caught by a real surprise.

I would have been better prepared to mentally process this if I had experienced this as a child in the school system at one level or another. However, my first experience with this was as a young adult. I was at a social occasion and was asked by a female (Filipina) about my nationality – was I Filipino? I replied in the affirmative that I was as

I had always done given that psychologically I had selected this as the ethnicity I chose to associate myself and be associated with. I was asked further if I was "pure" Filipino to which I responded that my mother was Irish. The person went on to exclaim in what I perceived to be a demeaning fashion, "Oh, you are not a "real" Filipino! This reaction I experienced on a number of similar occasions. During a conversation with my cousin, a Filipino – Mexican mestizo I shared this experience. My cousin who lives in southern California and a pastor of his own church related to me that he had a similar experience at a bank with a bank teller while depositing money. He related that he was asked by the Filipina bank teller if he was of Filipino heritage to which he replied that he was - but was mestizo. The teller asked him if he spoke his dialect (Ilocano). When he replied that he was not fluent in the language the teller in an admonishing tone exclaimed "Oh, you are not a real Filipino!". Needless to say, even as a "man of the cloth", he was dismayed by the comment, to say the least.

I had a similar experience with the exception that the person asked me in a bit of broken English if I "speak the language". I replied I did not (without explanation as to why) to which she exclaimed, "ah you are not a real Filipino!" I simply shook my head, chuckled to myself and went on my way. Incidentally, this is not the only such incident to, occur, there have been other, I may go further into analyzing this behavior and intent another book at a later date. I would like to think that the intent was not one of intended insult but of simple ignorance of how that phrase is interpreted; in actuality, as a phrase of insult by the perceiver. At some point, I would like to get the opportunity to discuss the language and cultural implication with a Filipino philosophical doctor in language and culture for more clarity and understanding.

Another Form of Prejudice in the Real Estate Business

For several years after retirement from civil service, I worked full time as a Broker-Associate for a private real estate company listing and selling real estate. Using the skills I learned over the years, I was able to do very well and was recognized and honored as Top Listing Agent of the Year for two years in a row. I was very effective at listing properties, single family and income property as well in Bakersfield, California a very conservative town. I always felt recognizable tension between "old guard" white real estate practitioners as well as real estate practitioners of color. A goodly number of real estate businesses were owned and/or operated by minorities. In the town, there were a significant number of brown sales agents as well as brown owned real estate brokerages as well. Standing out among peers as an aggressive and successful "Realtor" with the Bakersfield Association of Realtors" with the additional Real Estate Designation of GRI (Graduate - Realtor Institute), and on television nightly via our sub-association, I enjoyed my interactions with all of my real estate business peers, associates and competitors as well. I was fortunate to work in a brokerage owned by a very dynamic, knowledgeable and experienced female Real Estate Broker/Owner who was well known for not tolerating "baloney" from anyone. About the only "left field" label our office has was that of being referred to as the "Believers". Sometime this comment would come out of the most unexpected places. Being spiritual person and very familiar with church and religious faith however, I viewed the label as a compliment and it always brought a smile to my face.

Aside from the normal possibility of discrimination due to being brown in a conservative community, I found another element of discrimination as a Real Estate listing agent; that of being a male agent. It was my opinion that when it came to competing for the "Listing" agreement to represent the seller in selling a property, I would find that in cases where I was not personally known by the sellers and male owners "wore the pants" in the family, I would often lose out on listing a property to the attractive female agent. Not only did I lose the listing opportunity, other females who interviewed with the seller with "less" personality or in some cases who were of color, would lose out on the listing as well. I concluded my opinion on this to be valid after discussing the dynamics with the other agents and when, some years later after such competition for a listing, I accidently ran into an ex-wife of a couple who, with her husband, had interviewed me to list their property for sale. It was she that shared with me that she felt I was the most qualified and professional but that her ex-husband wanted to engage respective female agent as he was "uncomfortable" with me. She was quick to say that he wasn't thinking with the "right head". You can't win them all, but "knowing the truth can set you free".

Elements of American Discrimination Suffered by Father Manifests itself in Many Ways

However, as a matter of reasoning, I should elaborate that I do know that from my father's viewpoint, he did not see a benefit for his children to learn the language of the Filipino. In his mind he did not want me to be a Filipino but an American in as many ways as possible. I can only empathize with my father and his many experiences over the years trying to learn in a haphazard way, the correct pronunciation of words, meanings of phrases and colloquialisms of the English language. I can only imagine the giggles, laughs and wonderments expressed by his Caucasian classmate in classes while attending four years of Bible College in San Francisco, a man truly out of his element. I am amazed by the lack of sensitivity by many of the modern Filipinos in modern America to the experiences of early Filipino immigrants to the United States and the various forms and element of ridicule so many of them faced in their daily live trying to become "Americans". I am thus truly bewildered by the impact these experiences of my father and the wave of migrant Filipinos of the pre-bridge generation (the 1920, 30's 40's) had on me and other members of the "bridge" generation. I am very often still devastated by the perceived insensitivity many modern Filipinos have and exhibit for the many tremendous difficulties and degradations of vintage Filipinos experienced in their quest to become Americans. I am privileged to know of them listening to the many Filipinos associates of my father as over time they shared their experience with each other to encourage one another to continue the plight and struggle they experienced raising family and participating in the American dream. Now I as I reflect back on American history, I know that each wave of

European, Asian and African migrants experienced a correlated hostility from Americans that is to be put in perspective

The ridicule, mocking and scorn suffered by my father and other Filipino migrants of his generation is akin to attitudes I experienced as a youth when I was in school from uppity Caucasian students despite my naivete in not taking it to seriously. Their response to my mixed Caucasian-Filipino racial mixture and brown skin seemed to be one of shame on my behalf for me being the opposite of an Epiphany or divine revelation but another mixed ace freak of evolution of some kind! At the time, I did not understand it. Now I think – Really!!!??? Now I have grown; proud of my heritage and comfortable with my uniqueness and even fortunate to be different.

PART VIII

Resolving Prejudice and Discrimination – Coming to Terms

Discrimination and Where am I now on the issue of Prejudice? Fast - Forward

It has taken me a long time to get over the personal insecurities and sensitivities relative to inequality, disappointments and self-worthiness doubts about my value in American society as a Filipino-Caucasian (Northern European) mestizo.

I have had to work hard in so many different ways to put unpleasantries behind me or at least to the side. I find that financial equality if not superiority is the one element and achievement that gives me comfort. In that sense, I can understand that more is better. I have also found that putting racial unpleasantries behind me worked best if I was able to identify specific areas or ways in which I felt the burden of discrimination and the types of discrimination I was encountering. For example, did I find myself reacting to a single isolated instance of discrimination from an individual or was I encountering a broad stereotypical precept inherent in Americans of the white race. Where discrimination was occurring and projected toward me from an individual whether observed due to their personal attitude, real or imagined, or by an act or of unkindness or behavior, I found (because I wanted to) that there were more often than not, constructive ways to meet and mitigate the act or threat. In my case, I was only able to do this because I had identified my personally perceived inadequacies earlier in life and no longer had a need to become angry to justify harsh words and even aggressive behavior. I earlier spoke of achieving perceptions of mental superiority, but I also alluded to the need for achieving comparative financial superiority and independence. I found that for me, in my own mind, the possession of a Master Degree was sufficient enough for me. The combined possession of these two elements contributed greatly to me in validating my self-concept in the area of personal achievement and equality. Successfully mitigating the discriminatory situation or attitude I rationalized in my own mind, would be the true test of my equality. The important idea here is that because of these to elements of personal achievement, I no longer had a license to lash out in whatever way I might have because almost universally, professionals and people of means are in control of their life and world. To do otherwise and act out would be giving control over me and the outcome to the offender; I did not want to do that.

Unfortunately, because I did possess visible elements of personal and professional success I found I had to work very hard on being "just one of the guys" on occasion. Eventually, I found that in the long run, just being yourself and genuinely caring about your friend and those who may not have what you do is the best thing to do. In the long run, if you are sincere, and they want to be your friend, they will do so. If they do not, no amount of kindness, effort or understanding will change them or make a difference. I do have to add here that I also had a struggle. In this case, "water seeks its own level" as its attributed to an old Chinese proverb. Move on and do not invite another struggle into your life by trying to manage someone else's demons.

There are some mestizos who are trying or have tried to resolve feelings of inadequacy or anxieties brought on by living with discrimination and other individual issues. I have several acquaintances, even at this age, who see a counselor or therapist regularly or as needed. In such cases, just as in the case of divorce or death where one loses a partner it might be necessary for an individual to seek professional counselling services in order to get beyond personal anxieties and perceived inadequacies brought on by discrimination. I was fortunate to be in a career surrounded by many in professional fields where I was able to share concerns and solve problems and challenges. I tended to work on resolution of conflicts and inequality on my own. I believe I did a pretty fair job of accomplishing that. However, and this is a necessary caveat – I do believe that if one has issues and is having even a little difficulty with them, the "right" professional counselor or encounter situation will facilitate getting to the root issue quicker and moving more expeditiously toward the right tools and focused resolution.

An Experience and Advice That Could Save Your Life - Bridge Generation Individuals of Mixed Cultures Especially

I will say that on one occasion, when I thought I had my life together but, in fact had not - a friend encouraged me to visit a counselor. My friend told me that the very first time he visited a counselor, whom he referred me to, concerning an eminent divorce he was going through, that had felt like the weight of the world was lifted off of his shoulders. I was going through the same kind of marital situation as he and felt I was maneuvering through life walking like my head was under water. I was a manager, had to deal with organizational complexities, problem situations and problem people. I needed to get my act together and quickly. Despite feeling and maybe even knowing that I certainly needed to counsel with someone, I might not have gone so quickly except that I was aware of a higherup in my line of work that had taken his own life after seemingly unresolvable relationship conflict. I always felt bad for him in that, of all the people around him, and most likely a goodly number of "leg hangers" aka" groupies". For in that moment of need, I had concluded that he could not find the right person with a moment to spare to talk to him or guide him through his dilemma. I know it is more complex that that but more than once I have asked myself, in that moment of need, where are your friends when you really need them??? While I did not have a feeling of hurting myself, I was more than a little devasted by, what many divorcees experience as the feeling of failure after trying so hard at a subsequent relationship and expecting such good results. There are a lot of other factors involved in this dissolution dilemma process also. I did take my friends advice and do not mind sharing with anyone who needs a hand through life, that seeking counseling (from a "good" counselor - yes there are good and there are not so effective or even non-ethical) is an admirable thing to do. I can co-sign my friend's assessment of the weight of the world being lifted off of your shoulders almost immediately. This process has a dynamics all its own: this is not the place for the discussion. However, I must say that as a first generation Filipino-Caucasian, I (and perhaps we as a group) do not fully understand the innuendos and social dynamics of the society and sometimes sub-organizations in which we function. Don't feel too proud or too unimportant to delay calling anyone or seeking a professional referral if you are feeling under-valued or that life or a situation is hopeless. Counselling may not have been readily available for the Filipino immigrants of the 1920's through the 60's, but help is available now for stresses and life dilemmas - seek it, Demand it. When I was young, my mother had a saying she would share with me when I was feeling let down by a friend: A friend in need, is a friend indeed!" For those of us who have a spiritual background, reaching out in prayer is a good way for many to start issue resolution

Situations of prejudice occur but I am now prepared to accept them and resolve them without psychic harm or allowing them to ruin my wonderful life. Somewhat relatively recently I accompanied a Caucasian teacher who traveled in a somewhat uppity crowd and an ex-husband who was president of a well-known university, to a Christmas dinner. I got the word later that the gentlemen there shared with her indirectly that they did not think I was "right" for her. Had I encountered this situation earlier in life when I was less accomplished and affluent, I would have felt bad about it. Because of the attractiveness and social status of the individual, I felt I did recognize at work simultaneously, prejudice* and jealousy at work at the same time. However, because of my many experiences, accomplishments, psychological and emotional growth I was able to analyze the situation and put the incident and people in "proper context" and end it with a laugh.

I worked very hard to prove myself worthy of equity with other white Americans and to transcend into the American middle socio-economic class. It is relatively easy to break out of the confines of the lower economic class in America though it doesn't come easily; it does take effort, determination, some knowledge and a good deal of people skills. Perhaps, my next book will address the experiences and methods of achieving this. Breaking out of the lower or even middle social class, that's a little more difficult and the lines very blurred, the labels very gray in my opinion. According to commonly accepted and established

American sociological theory however, a non-white or WASP (white Anglo-Saxon protestant) cannot become a member of the American upper-class. That is a dream I have however and a topic for me to deal with from my point of view in another writing however. * *(In the statement above, I recognize that I use the common term "prejudice" which is more or less inaccurate as "pre-judgement" is out of context here. In reality what I observed was more an emotion of envy, disdain and jealousy all in one; an element so common in Caucasian Americans where the devil rises up on the Caucasians shoulder to say "Why should that brown bastard have what I want?" I say this, because, I have been in company of some very gorgeous Caucasian and other women and thus, have seen this dynamics at play on numerous occasions. I am sure this dynamics played itself out on many occasions for Filipino immigrants (1920's 30's and 40's) – some of our forefathers in their day at Saturday night ballroom dances.)*

Fast Forwarding from Childhood to the Autumn of Life and Beyond

There have been so many times when I have reassured myself with the affirmation that I am so blessed and happy to be me, as I am, and that I wouldn't want to trade places with anyone else. There are some things I would have done differently and would have made some better choices. I would have started earlier making better choices but I wouldn't have changed much.

I feel I have still not fully overcome the impact of prejudice and particularly racial prejudice. I owe whatever successes I have experienced on that journey to many, many people around me from the church I attended, my relatives, my many friends from all ethnicities, cultures, (social and intimate); my neighbors, community organizations, work peers, educators, et al. These reflections lend themselves to the makings of another great story of ups and downs, social and economic dynamics as well as dissection and application of the behavioral science concepts that apply to them.

As I continue on my life's journey, each day, I feel I am better off mentally than the day before and feel I have had a full and acceptably rewarding life. As I lose friends and associates unpredictably, due to "natural causes", old age, health challenges or accidents, I more and more, realize that my time and that of my associates is limited. I still feel that there is a lot I would like to get done and a shorter time than I would like to get it all done. I feel that I, as a first generation Filipino-Caucasian American, (and that perhaps others in my position) had to spend a lot of my life just establishing an American family heritage in America. I am concerned that I have a perception that my sons, regardless of their generational removal from initial immigration to America, do not seem to me, to feel like "real" Americans yet. Though there seems to be a number of areas where the syndrome of "*herd assimilation*" has taken hold, there still seems to be a number of areas where it has not taken hold and cannot be taken for granted. That remaining displacement seems to be based on what could be considered, in my opinion, the seeming curse of skin color or more specifically, Americans living in brown skin. I feel that based on my life experience there are a number of factors that need to come together for an American in brown skin in order for he or she to become accepted by the faction of "Americans" that I have repeatedly discussed throughout this life manuscript, (now book) as a real American.

I feel that as generations evolve in America and dissimilarities less pronounced or identifiable, and in many cases, in time disappear, this discussion and topic of discrimination against the Filipino-Caucasian American mestizos will truly be historical - as historical as tyrannosaurus rex and dinosaurs. This will likely be the reality of hundreds of years off into the future, assuming that our society survives the current Corvid 19 virus, imminent social disruption and plagues of the future that are currently even more unimaginably devastating to our society as we know it.

Fast Forwarding from Childhood to the Autumn of Life and Beyond

There are some from current generations of Filipino descent I have talked with, who seem shocked by the reality of harsh treatment experienced by Filipinos who migrated to America in the 1920, 30's and even the 1940's. I walk away from these conversations concluding that these people would probably rather not think about the matter, that if they don't think too hard about it, they don't have to acknowledge that it ever existed, or admit that they despite wearing designer clothes and driving expensive care, are not of a higher status among "Americans" than those of us who did experience discrimination. To think about the reality of the prejudice and mistreatment seems to interfere with their cozy relationships with Caucasians who they have come to trust as friends and not question their friend's premise on Filipinos in American Society. This writing is not intended to cause doubt and riffs between people of the Filipino heritage and their friends of all colors. It is intended to highlight the past challenges and connect to the present and future in a historical and cautionary way. Based on my past experiences in American society, this work is not intended to have the reader presume that real change has occurred and there is no more to be done - fait accompli! Emphatically No! Immigrants of Filipino descent and their mestizo children have survived, and in many cases, began to flourish personally, culturally, professionally and socio-economically. However, in many overt cases and subliminally as well, my children of Filipino descent cannot assume that because they are not confronted almost daily with racial epitaphs and slurs and are seemingly friends with "higher" class kids and families, they can innocently and safely conclude that they are honest and truly accepted as a true-blue part of the American landscape. Be cautious, on *guard* and strong enough to take the good with the bad, if and when, the American ugly snake of racism comes out from under the rock and raises it's ugly head to strike at you - you of Filipino-Caucasian heritage. I will leave this with the final Caveat of caution.

Final Caveat: Actions speak louder than words. Apply this as you may.

Example: A Caucasian friend who belongs to a local country club delighted in telling me how excited he would be to have me join him for a round of golf at his country club and that he would invite me soon! That was four years ago, I see him often; I am still waiting for the T-off time notification. At some point, I will conclude, if I haven't already, that he "spoke with forked tongue" maybe just to appear benevolent and unbiased in front of others - or to me - lol. Coincidently, I have a Filipino friend who invited me to play golf as a guest at his country club on numerous occasions and has done all he can to get me to come out to play; so many times in fact, that I could not possibly keep that kind of a golfing schedule. Again, actions speak louder than words!

Context and Environment May Make a Difference

As this book goes in to final draft, I had the unfortunate experience of sharing in the final farewell of a dear friend's mother whom I had come to appreciate as almost my own as a friend's mother could be. In the environment and in attendance were approximately sixty people. Given the thesis of this book I looked around at demographic of the attendees a by now you, the reader, assumes I would be. I surmised that approximately six of those present including myself were people of color. I must say that during this period of time I perceive no feelings of reservation in interaction with the attendees and appreciated the sincerity of conversation, acceptance and camaraderie on our collective loss. I am thankful for that rewarding experience and gift of this blessing of inclusion given by the departed.

There have been so many times when I have reassured myself with the affirmation that I am so blessed and happy to be me as I am and that I wouldn't want to trade places with anyone else.

Hometown Workplace Realities
Observed in Today's World

On my recent return to Stockton California I visited a fast-food establishment close to my home for something quick, a breakfast, lunch or dinner sandwich. It dawned on me that surprisingly, the counter service members were often of Filipino descent. I thought – this is a truly different environmental experience compared to my experiences in other parts of in California, America and the world. I thought to myself – Oh, How wonderful! This is what it's like to be home! Here people look like me and my ancestry here seems quite common. I know the counter help had not a clue to my quite smile and expression of thanks and appreciation but my feeling of resolve and appreciation was not easily explainable within myself either. I can only commit to further appreciation and acknowledgement of what my father started so many years ago on the shores of California and his quest to contribute to America, and his thanks for finally being an American.

I asked myself how this change had come about and such seeming transition in community composition had occurred. I realized that I had been away so long and the evolution of the community had gone on without me. Subsequently my thoughts reflected back to the time I returned from military service and subsequently joined a career with the California Department of Corrections right out of the Stockton community and that I had been essentially absent from the community for close to 50 years. I ask myself, why is it people never hit the lottery until they are too old to enjoy it? I think back to other communities I worked in and lived in and think – How different my home community is now from those others and how wonderful to finally return home where many reflect my ancestry here in America!!!!

.

Epilogue

The author has many life-experiences and has shared insight into many of them here. The author plans to pursue additional writings

As I look around the community upon my return, and in my opinion, I have not found what I consider an equitable representation of Filipino, Filipino-Caucasian Mestizo or other Asian representation as heads of local cities or county government over the many years since I had been gone. I do hope to see this perception and reality improve. I look at each young Pinoy or Pinay I encounter in the community and I think, maybe this will be our future first Filipino Mayor, City Manager, Chief of Police, Sheriff, District Attorney, Filipino community mentor, etcetera. I was very pleasantly surprised recently that while eating at a Hawaiian food restaurant, I observed a small group of Filipino and Asian Stockton Police Officers stopping for a quick lunch in-route to a special assignment. I hope to see them eventually rise to Line Command positions at some time in the future.

As this book goes into publication the United States is in the grips of a health crisis due to the Corvid 19 worldwide pandemic and national civil unrest due to the death of a black man in police custody in Minneapolis, Minnesota. Many city mayors and governors throughout the nation, are in the news and interviewed; many black, some brown. However, none, I have viewed on national news interviews watching almost twenty-four hours a day, thus far, appear to be of Filipino or Asian heritage which I personally found disappointing. I hope to see that perception and/or reality change in my life-time.

Yes, opportunities abound in the United States and the brown-skinned Filipino Mestizos are now comparatively and seemingly, well insulated from the past at-will aggressive, overt insults of Caucasians and the general public while pursuing their meaningful destiny. These civil rights protections seem to allow the Filipino-Caucasian the opportunity to exercise freedoms, self-expression and entrance into almost all venues he or she may choose without fear of challenge, verbal insults, intimidation and bullying. I am also excited and my spirit buoyed by the achievements of my Filipino-Caucasian Mestizos I have become aware of and continue to recognize in the community of my birth.

Authors Parents Final Resting Place - Rural Cemetery, Stockton Calif.
Alfonso Agdeppa Fillon, Sinait Illocus Sur P. I.
Mary Kirkpatrick Fillon, Alton, Illinois USA

MY HEROES AND SUPPORT

Family Photo

Left to Right: Sofia, Grand-daughter, Al Fillon- Grandfather, Alejandro, Grandson, Alfonso,
Son and Father of Children   Missing: Patty Solis-Fillon Daughter-In-Law, Mother of Children
and Wife of Son Alfonso

Mary Ellen Kirkpatrick Fillon
Mother of Author
Aug. 6, 1915 - Mar. 8, 2000

Author Al Fillon, Division Manager - Criminal Justice,
and Emergency Services and Security Management Division,
(circa 2006) pictured with Dr. David Baker, College President

Author Experiences - Unabridged

The author has many life-experiences and has shared insight into many of them here. The author plans to pursue additional writings including a series of novels relative to working in the criminal justice system over 40 years and the many types of daily situations one encounters in daily operations and characteristic inherent in the people that operate within that system both as overseers and the clientele. The characters themselves however, are expected to be fictional. The first in the "Dirty Warden" Series, already being written, is expected to be published within the year and takes you inside the walls and in the community into a world of intrigue, deceit, life and death beyond imagination.

Alfonso K. Fillon was born in 1946 in a small valley town of Stockton, California. His family lived in Stockton's southside, a patchwork of poor, multiracial neighborhoods whose wage earners were low-income, blue collar workers or on welfare. Southside neighborhood homes were usually of substandard architecture, ill-kept and interspersed with trailer homes and unpaved driveways. This setting provided a foundation for challenge and doubt in the minds of many that the youth from these neighborhoods would ever attend college, find important, well-paid employment or even become valuable and productive citizens. But that is exactly what many of these youths did just that, attain lofty goals, acquire fame and fortune despite the economic, cultural, racial and language barriers they had to overcome! This is the story of how one youth, a son of a Filipino immigrant overcame the stigma of living in Stockton's southside and overcame an overwhelming barrage of racial discrimination against those of Filipino, heritage, and social conflict, and make the system work for him. He tells a story of how he was able to heals scars of discrimination and achieve a respectable level of social status, professional success and financial comfort.

Mr. Fillon attended Colleges in California attaining an Associate of Arts Degree at of Stockton's San Joaquin Delta College (Social Science 69'), a Bachelor of Arts in Criminal Justice Administration at Calif. State University–San Bernardino and a Master of Public Administration from Calif. State University – Bakersfield. He possesses a Community College Teaching Credential in Public Services and Administration, has taught for community colleges classes and was a Program Manager and Division Manager over Corrections, Police Sciences and Emergency Services Departments at San Joaquin Valley College, taught Criminal Justice Classes for Santa Barbara Business College. He has Federal Emergency Management Certs for: Incident Command, Emergency Operations Management and Operations, Emergency Command in Hospitals, Schools and Health Care Organizations and Hospitals, Law Enforcement and Incident Command Systems for Law Enforcement and Tribal Communities. He has taught Laws of Arrest, Search and Seizure for various agencies. Mr. Fillon has completed Designated Courses of the International Assoc for Health Care and Security (IAHSS) Basic, Supervisory, Advanced Certifications for Health Care Security and Safety.

Mr. Fillon began his career with the California Department of Corrections at Deuel Vocational Institution – Tracy California in 1968 and retiring in 2000 after a 32 plus year career. During employment with CDCR Mr. Fillon worked in departmental positions from at Prisons throughout California 33 prisons system from Correctional Officer to Interim Warden at Salinas Valley State Prison, Monterey, County with six years of his career was as a Parole Administrator in Command of State Parole Operations, Field Services and Law Enforcement Liaison in Orange, San Bernardino, Riverside, San Diego, Imperial and East Los Angeles County with responsibility for operation of Parole Offices & Community Rehabilitation Facilities with 22,000 parolees in community supervision.

Mr. Fillon's also functioned as a Team Leader with Corrections' Headquarters Emergency Operations Unit responsible for assessment and formulation of prison emergency readiness throughout the State of California which included Service Systems Interruptions, Riot Control and Containment, Escape, Prevention and Recovery, Medical/Dental Triage, Personnel Trauma, Public Information and Personnel Systems Management, Emergency Command Conduct, Protocol and Procedures including Hostage Negotiations, SERT and Sniper Deployment Tactics, etc;. Mr. Fillon is a Security Consultant, an Expert Witness on Corrections Operations, Management, Security, Criminal and Death Penalty Defense. He has also worked Casino/Resort/Hotel Security and as a Private Prisons Warden.

Mr. Fillon is a licensed Real Estate Broker with GRI designation, a top Listing Agent; has served on numerous Civic and Boards, held Executive positions with public service associations and fraternal lodges. He is an active member of the Moose Lodge, Elks Lodge and Past Worthy President Fraternal Order of Eagles. He is particular proud to have served on the Board of Directors of the Stockton Associated Filipino Organizations Inc, in Stockton, Ca. which is the adopted American town of his father and in which he was raised, the Retired Public Employees Association (California) and a member of Filipino American National Historical Society (FANHS), Stockton Chapter.

He is a Viet Nam Veteran having served with U. S. Naval Amphibious operations with an Honorable Discharge. He now resides in Bakersfield, California.

Printed in the United States
By Bookmasters